Praise for 'The FOG'

"As an Author, I have delved into the modern science of the Holy Shroud supporting the writings of the Gospels on the historical Jesus of Nazareth. I was, therefore, profoundly moved by this book by Sherry Turner which goes into elements of modern science that compliment and help us more deeply understand the words of the Bible. I was touched by her scholarly work and highly recommend this wonderful book to all."

-John C. Iannone, Author/Speaker

The FOG, The Face Of God

By Sherry Turner

*Author photo courtesy of Jeanine Inda

*Quotes from scripture were all taken from the NIV Study Bible, unless otherwise denoted. *The NIV Study Bible*. Grand Rapids, MI: Zondervan Pub. House, 1995. Print

The FOG

The Face Of God

By Sherry Turner

- Contents -

"If my people, who are called by my name, will humble themselves and pray and seek my face and turn from their wicked ways, then I will hear from heaven and will forgive their sin and will heal their land."

2 Chronicles 7:14

- *Note from the Author* -

"For it is not the one who commends himself who is approved, but the one whom the Lord commends." 2 Corinthians 10:18

Please know I do not even begin to think that I have any authority to write on this – the holiest of topics – except for that which God has gifted to me by His Spirit.

I had been working for a large real estate company in the Orlando area, while also dealing with the challenges of raising my two children as a single parent. Having been on my own for seven years, I fully understood the daily struggles of balancing "breadwinning" in the workforce and homemaking/child rearing in the home. (As single mothers we unknowingly take on the curses for both the man and the woman of original sin.) The earth becomes difficult for us to toil, work becomes laborious, *and* we feel the pain and discomfort in childbearing. (-from Genesis 3)

As if this wasn't enough, early in the year of 2009, I suffered a neck injury that nearly took my life. About a month following the injury I had a minor stroke – or a "Transient Ischemic Attack," as the medical world calls it. My neurosurgeon advised that I may be at risk for having a major stroke, and that he had lost a patient due to very similar circumstances. I was told it was possible that within the next few months I could have a severe stroke as well.

The Face of God 6

After digesting this information and wrestling with God over fears about death and leaving my loved ones (especially my children), I finally came to a place of peace knowing where I would be going if that happened, and a place of comfort in knowing that Jesus would keep my children safe until they reached that same destination.

But it was then that I was given a drastic sense of urgency to get this book (that I knew God had given me) out of my head and onto paper. I felt as if it could possibly die with my brain, and the world would never know what the Lord had done and what He had revealed to me!

I first wrote letters to my babies (that could be read to them if I were to pass), explaining to them where their mommy was, that everything was okay, and how they should follow God's commandments, and above all believe Jesus in order to live wonderful lives here, resting assured that they would see me again when it was their time to be reunited with the Lord.

And then I began to write this book. I had no idea what I was getting into and how much time it would really take!

Thankfully, that major stroke never hit me, but as a complication from the injury I developed cardiovascular problems that led to heart failure – essentially ensuring that for the next two years at least, I would be too tired to resume the social life I had once revered, and I would want nothing more than time to lie in bed and write this book. I eventually learned not to complain, as it became clear that God uses even painful or traumatic events for His greater purposes. As scripture says, I learned to be grateful in all things.

But then I questioned: Why me? Why didn't God use someone who was already a writer by trade, or someone who was famous or significant in some way to give the message in this book to the world? And why did He allow me to suffer through the pain, the fatigue, and the fear I went through to ensure I would write this book?

Two answers became clear:

One, after all that the Lord had done for me in the past, He knew I had surrendered myself to Him out of sheer gratitude. I had repeatedly told God that my life was His to use. And He knew that although I was stubborn, my heart was loyal.

And two, if any other author had written this book, for whatever reason, you might not have picked it up.

But here you are reading it. Whatever channels God used to deliver it through, it somehow got into your hands. He knows what He is doing. He wanted you. And He used me to get to you. I'm okay with that. In fact, I'm more than okay with that. You are one of God's children, and He loves you.

God 'wants all men to be saved and come to a knowledge of the truth.' 1 Timothy 2:4

Part of that truth is that the effects of our behaviors in this fallen world – having been led and fed by the lies of the enemy – will be culminating in a time of chaos and suffering at its fullest. Yet God has not forsaken His children. For those He has called, there will be a rebirth of a new heaven and a new world not based under the authority of lies, but founded in love and in the truth. The path to becoming a part of that new world is so truly amazing, and is as perfect as the creation itself.

Thank you again for taking the time to read this and for sharing it with those you love and care about as well.

"Surely you have heard about the administration of God's grace that was given to me for you, that is, the mystery made known to me by revelation, as I have already written briefly. In reading this then, you will be able to understand my insight into the mystery of Christ, which was not made known to men in other generations as it has now been revealed by the Spirit to God's holy apostles and prophets." Ephesians 3: 2-5

- *Acknowledgments* -

I am so grateful to Dr. Robert Masson, Dr. Robert Dalton, Dr. Tony Shydohub, Dr. James Scelfo, and Dr. Gary Allen in Orlando for their wisdom and care of my physical health. I also wish to express much appreciation and respect to Pastor Joe Saragusa and the people of Celebrate Church, (now The Crossing Church) in Celebration, Florida, where I first heard the Good News and the truth of God in a way that made sense to me. I truly cannot thank you enough for caring about my spiritual health.

I also thank the Rev. Patrick Wrisley, the Rev. Dr. William A. Lewis, and the people of the Community Presbyterian Church in Celebration for their wonderful persistence in providing a safe place to learn about the Bible and to enjoy much needed fellowship. I especially appreciate this church for baptizing me and my babies.

I'm so thankful to all of the other amazing churches and church leaders in my town and around the globe through whom the word of God also thankfully reached me, including Dr. David Uth -Senior Pastor of First Baptist Orlando, Dr. Joel C. Hunter -Senior Pastor of Northland Church, Pastor Greg Dumas and Pastor Tim Ingram -Senior and Campus Pastors of The Crossing Church, Father Gregory Parkes -Pastor of Corpus Christi Catholic Church, Pastor Joseph Wamack of the Celebration Adventist Church and many others. Thank you for your presence and your perseverance. Thank you for not growing weary in your efforts to help reach the lost amongst us.

I also am grateful to Eileen Wilson, Marissa Crawford, Maggie Paedae, the Kapustas and the Heart's Truth ministry, to the Goads, to Leah Sams, Ashley Servine,

Heather Robbins, Pam Osorio, Meg Sweeney, Melanie Scott, Kristen Tate and the women of MOPS, to Carolyn Pankalla and her ministry, to John Iannone for his study of the Holy Shroud, to Lynde and Mark Jones and the team of Celebrate Recovery leaders around the country, to Sarah Trollinger and all of the people who serve at the House of Hope, to Rick Warren, Joel Osteen, Kay Arthur, Beth Moore, Noel Jones, Michelle McKinney Hammond and so many others. My thanks to each of you who are in this world writing, working, helping, sharing and continuing to work out your salvations. You serve as an inspiration with your tireless efforts to spread the light and the hope of God in our hurting world. Thank you for all you do. Thank you also to Sharon Symonette, Edgardo Cordero and Lori Annen for the use of their beautiful faces on the cover. And thank you so much Amy Owen, Brenda Hart, Karen Kuers, Mac Autrey, Bob Spraker, Gregory E. Shultz, Jonathan Janis, James Cochran and Al Valentino III for your support in bringing this project to life. I thank the Lord for allowing me to be a part of your lives. And I thank God for my family, my mom -Karole Turner, dad -Woodrow Wilson Turner Jr. and step mom - Trudy Weatherholtz Turner, my siblings and their spouses - Karen Turner and John Mark Power, and Bryan and Catherine Turner, and my Aunts, Uncles, cousins, nieces and extended relatives... I'm so grateful for such a fun and wonderful family!

Thank you to my children Samantha and Mason for being shining lights, brave in this big world, where their faith in God shines and their joy is contagious.

And to all of my dear sisters and brothers in Christ, thank you for your support and love. Keep on believing.

The Face of God 12

The Face of God 13

- Introduction -

"An angel of the Lord appeared to him in a dream and said, "Joseph son of David, do not be afraid to take Mary home as your wife, because what is conceived in her is from the Holy Spirit. She will give birth to a son, and you are to give him the name Jesus, because he will save his people from their sins." – Matthew 1:20

We once named our children based on the meanings of the names themselves. A person's name signified their intended purpose, or the events surrounding their birth, or something of significance which their life represented. Although this practice has largely given way to naming conventions that seem to carry no inherent meanings, there still exists a correlation that can be recognized between a person's name and their ultimate persona. Somewhat like the Pygmalion effect coined by Robert Rosenthal wherein children labeled as "intellectual bloomers" really *did* succeed, studies show that the names given to our children will act as labels which subconsciously or consciously help determine how they are perceived by themselves and others. These perceptions will manifest in behaviors the name bearer displays as well as behaviors others direct towards them, further solidifying the effect of their namesake. What appears to be some sort of self- fulfilling prophesy emerges as the name given bears its meaning.

By chapter seven of this book we will see this to be true of not only names, but of words in general. And by chapter nine we will see the revelation of the meaning of the highest of names, that which is coming to fruition in the name Jesus Christ.

It actually surprised me to learn that the meaning of the name Jesus, or "Yahwe" in Hebrew, is 'The Lord Saves.' But that was before I understood the nature of our fallen world, the *cyclical* nature of our interaction with the world, and the ultimate ending of all that has attached itself to our world. But now, it all makes sense. The Lord saves. He saves us as we live, and He saves us in the end.

From a scientific perspective we will see not only how His life saves all those who are held in captivity – by whomever or whatever they are enslaved to – but also how being covered by the astounding power behind His name actually saves us from the impending condemnation of the world as we know it. It's a lot to take in, so buckle up when you're ready!

Up until now, much of what spiritual leaders throughout history have preached has required complete leaps of faith to truly believe. Now – although we as humans still cannot fully comprehend it all, and faith is still the ultimate outcome required of us – the latest findings in science can help us to overcome hurdles we once had to truly believing and understanding the spiritual principles that Jesus himself explained.

Depending on your knowledge of psychology, chemistry and physics, some of the ideas in this book may be difficult to assimilate. Our brains build new connections between cells each time we learn something new. It is easier for us to integrate material if we already have pathways between brain cells, called a "framework" in place. However, if the concepts are completely new, with no frame of reference upon which we can build, we have to physically create new pathways to connect brain cells. The older we are, the more difficult this can seem, so I ask that you remain patient.

In order to get all of the readers "on the same page," so to speak, we will be laying down a foundation chapter by chapter in order to build the framework of understanding necessary for integrating the deeper concepts we will later address. I hope you will take the time to read and digest each chapter so that you will be able to "see" what it is that God has shared with me that is so important for us to know for our future.

According to the contributors of the documentary *What the Bleep do We Know,'* it has also been said that when Columbus' first ships reached North America, the natives had no frame of reference in their minds for what a "ship" in the water was; and that when they looked out at the horizon, despite the fact that ships were out there, they couldn't see them. It wasn't until the shaman noticed the rippling of the water created by their waves, and by remaining open in his thinking, that he searched to see what could be causing this effect.

After many attempts, growing connections in his brain each time, he was finally able to recognize that there were objects in the sea in front of them. The rest of the natives trusted the authority of the shaman and opened their minds as well, allowing them to grow to see the ships for themselves. [1]

As you read, I hope you will remain open in your mind to build upon each new framework, until you will be able to see things and understand this world through what will seem like a whole new lens.

In scripture, the apostle Paul tells us that when a person comes to believe in the word of God, it is like a veil is removed from their face, a veil that had been covering their vision; and that once it is removed, they can see clearly.

It is also at that point when others can clearly see something that had been hidden behind that veil. It is a face I have come to recognize and love. And it is why I titled this book *The Face of God*.

"Whenever anyone turns to the Lord, the veil is taken away…And we who with unveiled faces all reflect the Lord's glory, are being transformed into his likeness with ever increasing glory, which comes from the Lord, who is the Spirit."
2 Corinthians 3:8

1

- Chapter One -

Nikola Tesla, the inventor of the radio and one of the most brilliant electrical engineers the world has ever known, knew he was on to something huge with a phenomenon he witnessed in his New York City laboratory in the late 1800's. It was something of such enormous significance, he became obsessed with it, and spent the remainder of his life inventing, demonstrating, and devoting all of his talent to. According to many sources, Tesla actually started to exhibit pronounced symptoms of obsessive-compulsive disorder in the years following this amazing discovery. He apparently "became obsessed with the number three; he often felt compelled to walk around a block three times before entering a building and demanded a stack of three folded cloth napkins beside his plate at every meal." [1]

Something of eternal significance had been revealed to Nikola Tesla, but without knowing the Trinity of God and God's word, the truth of his powerful discovery eluded him.

According to many sources, the story of his discovery ended in him having to take a sledge hammer to his invention. Apparently, he had inadvertently created a small earthquake that shook the neighboring buildings to his New York City lab, and nearly took down his entire building!

Police came barreling into his lab just in time to see him destroy the miniature vibrating device that had created all of the damage.

This device was small enough to fit in a coat pocket, yet when tuned to specific vibration frequencies, it would cause other objects that were naturally oscillating at that frequency to vibrate as well. It was a device powerful enough to create an earthquake throughout all of Manhattan with nothing more than the resonant energy of its vibrations. This incredible discovery led Tesla to create numerous other experiments in mechanical and electrical versions of resonance. In his lab he became known for creating enormous artificial lightning storms that astounded his visitors. Although he may not have been the first to discover resonance, he was able to prove that the Earth is a conductor and he discovered that the resonant frequency of the Earth was approximately 8 hertz. [2]

During his life it was rumored that he had become overwhelmed with the powerful importance of what he had been studying, but neither he, nor anyone else, knew exactly why it was so important; until now. Over a hundred years later, God has finally revealed to us that this phenomenon Tesla recognized called "resonance" is actually an extremely significant part of *His* design to change the world as we know it.

More powerful than any manmade example Tesla could have dreamed of, God's presence in the realm of our physical world in all three forms of His Trinity at once will be the event that Tesla subconsciously knew would take place, and will be the most incredible demonstration of resonance ever.

To explain this we need to gain a basic understanding of some fundamental concepts in the sciences. Beginning with psychology and physiology, and working forward from there into physics and quantum physics, we will see how what once seemed impossible in this realm is actually just as Jesus explained it to be.

Psychology, the study of the human mind, is an evolving science. As we learn more about it, we open the door to understanding the marvelous works of our Creator in ways we could never have appreciated before. Social Psychology, the study of the human mind in relation to others, has gained considerable importance as we discover the inseparability of ourselves from our surroundings. And as the world through modern technology becomes more and more connected, the understanding of social psychology on a global scale becomes more and more valuable.

One of the most widely accepted theories of social psychology, known as "cognitive dissonance," is described as the tension we feel when our beliefs are in conflict with our actions or with new information or newer beliefs. The conflict between the two is uncomfortable in our minds, and leads to the production of feelings including guilt, anger and shame. In a subconscious effort to reduce this tension, we become motivated to alter our conflicting cognitions so that they become harmonious with one another. Psychologists can recognize individuals resorting to methods of denying, blaming or justifying in their attempt to reduce the tension of the dissonance between the conflicting beliefs or attitudes.

If that sounds confusing, take Aesop's fable about the fox and the sour grapes as one example of this. When the hungry fox sees grapes hanging from a tree, he wants them. But, finding that he cannot think of a way to reach them, he changes his attitude about the grapes and surmises that they must be rotten or sour anyway, relieving himself of the dissonance he felt for wanting something he could not have.

The truth is that when the Creator of the entire universe formed us, He included within us the knowledge of His will, His great plan, and all of His laws, deeply embedded within our souls. Scripture tells us **"His laws are in our hearts, written on our minds." (Hebrews 10:16.)** Yet, the world, from day one in our earthly bodies has told us a different story. We "see" things as they were not meant to be. We learn that society accepts things that contradict God's law, and we are told that that is okay. We are somehow subconsciously lied to from every angle.

I once thought if I were an alien traveling the universe and landed on Earth (somewhere in the United States), seeking to discover what life was all about here, I might peruse the local magazine stands to find out. After reviewing the majority of these periodicals, I would walk away thinking the goals of occupants of this planet must be to: (1) own a fast, loud car; (2) have muscle-bound bodies that all look alike; (3) have perfectly designed and furnished surroundings; (4) clothe themselves with only a certain quality and style of fabric; and (5) to achieve the perfect orgasm (although not necessarily in that order).

On a more serious note, while all these things are nice, it would seem to an outsider as though they are the most significant things in our world. Are these really the things the majority of us are chasing after? Is this what we really have our minds set on? As crazy as that now seems to me, beginning when we are children, *this* is much of what the world's culture teaches us and what many of us become driven by.

But the truth is that none of these things has any eternal significance. In the greater picture, none of them matter at all. Even we ourselves- our lives- are only significant to the degree for which they have been purposed in relationship to that which does have eternal meaning. And these 'things' only have meaning in the way they can be utilized for the fulfillment of God's purpose for our lives.

"In the beginning O Lord, you laid the foundations of the earth, and the heavens are the work of your hands. They will perish, but you remain; they will all wear out like a garment. You will roll them up like a robe; like a garment they will be changed. But you remain the same, and your years will never end."
Hebrews 1:11

Known as one of the wealthiest and wisest rulers ever to live, King Solomon devoted much of his time to observing the world and everything it had to offer us. After much consideration, he determined it all to be meaningless. **"Everything is meaningless." (Ecclesiastes 1:2)** He goes on to say nothing under the sun is new, it has all been done or said before, it is all just being repeated, and it is all a "meaningless chasing after the wind." The key phrase to note in his writings, however, is "under the sun," because thankfully, above the sun there *is* meaning. And the things we do or say or create here *do* have relevance in accordance with their relationship to that which does have meaning. [3]

You may not be there yet, but as we will see, it is only by our relationship to Christ that our lives and the happenings within and all around us make any sense. Apart from God's purpose, the things of the world that we chase after are like Solomon said: "a chasing after the wind."

However, the tension of cognitive dissonance is a real manifestation of our confusion here. And that tension will start to grow as somewhere in childhood, we begin to believe the world that these are the types of 'things' we should be aiming for and that these are what is important, contradicting what God has purposed for us, what is truly important and what deep inside, our souls already know. The fabric of our being knows one truth, but our minds begin to believe another. And so, as we succumb to believe the lies that have been handed down to us by the corruption of the world, and allow them to dictate our choices and actions, we fall short of our design and purpose, and we begin to feel the cognitive dissonance. It seems almost inevitable. As we live in conformity with the current world views, we allow ourselves to be led to do things that are against what we know deep in our hearts to be right. As scripture tells us, **"No servant can serve two masters... You cannot serve both God and money... What is highly valued among men is detestable in God's sight." (Luke 16:14)**

If the world teaches us that one way is right, won't we despise the other message? Yet we allow ourselves to get swept up in the rat race and to believe things that we know subconsciously in our deepest memory cells are not true. So the tension builds, and the drive to rid ourselves of it continues to produce even more behaviors and attitudes that cover us further with the shame and guilt we live under.

At a certain age, we all (hopefully) begin to recognize that the world is not right. We witness injustices, we see fighting and wars, natural disasters, poverty, hunger, abuse, failures, and we struggle with illnesses that seem to have no cure. As adults we begin to search for greater truths and understanding. Thankfully, we have valuable teachings at our disposal from spiritual leaders like the Dali Lama, Siddhartha the Buddha, and other wise leaders and prophets from the distant past through today. From them we learn many realities about the universe, the human condition, and social behaviors that benefit ourselves and others.

During my personal quest for the truth, I recognized all of these teachings to be extremely valuable, and I am so grateful for them. But even with all of this knowledge, I was still missing something. The tension was still there for me as my soul still felt scared, alone and lost. I was missing the love and the peace that I *now* know come only from the one living God, the Creator of it all. It was only when I finally aligned my beliefs with the words of the source of life itself that I was able to find that peace and hold onto it. Through meditation I believe we can experience glimpses of what the real source of peace feels like, but only by making an unbreakable connection to the source itself can we keep that peace with us as we continue to live and work in this fallen world. And what I found to be that unbreakable connection, was something that had been there all along, but because I had been blinded by the coverings of my selfishness, pride, guilt, shame, fear and the like, I couldn't see it, and therefore couldn't believe it.

Thankfully however, as scripture says, when one turns to the Lord, the veil is removed. In the moment of faith that I finally turned to God, and surrendered myself humbly to our Creator, and believed in His true design (witnessed over two thousand years ago, and with us since the creation itself), when I finally understood the truths of His laws and His words, and when I finally truly believed and accepted Jesus Christ as my own personal truth, *then* the dissonance was finally resolved. The spirits of shame and guilt, and the need to blame and justify were gone. I was freed from them.

At the time this happened for me, I didn't understand why – upon truly believing in Christ – I had been filled with such a powerful feeling of relief. It wasn't until later, looking back, that I was able to understand this psychological phenomenon occurring, and understand that from there forward, cognitive dissonance no longer disturbed me. The truth I believed in my mind from that moment forward matched the truth I was born with in my inner soul, written on my heart.

"Then you will know the truth, and the truth will set you free." (John 8:32)

When this happens for Christians, life is forever changed. We are freed from the future behaviors we would have continued. As scripture says, by his blood, our hearts are sprinkled clean from a guilty conscience, and we no longer have to justify our actions. We are justified by our faith in Him alone.

There is obviously more to it than just this, and we will be delving deeper into what is happening within and all around us as this change in our lives takes place. But in essence, when we truly believe in Jesus Christ and what He has done for us, the weight of the veil is lifted and the tension of the dissonance between what God created us to be and what we have been is removed. And, when we understand God's forgiveness and grace for all, we become aware of what we have done and why; we can step out of the darkness and into the light for the first time, open and unveiled, created in His image, with the uncovered Face of God.

"For God who said, 'Let light shine out of darkness,' made his light shine in our hearts to give us

the light of the knowledge of the glory of God in the face of Christ."
2 Corinthians 4:6

"Whoever believes in him is not condemned, but whoever does not believe stands condemned already because he has not believed in the name of God's one and only Son. This is the verdict; Light has come into the world, but men loved darkness instead of the light because their deeds were evil. Everyone who does evil hates the light, and will not come into the light for fear his deeds will be exposed. But whoever lives by the truth comes into the light, so that it may be seen plainly that what he has done has been done through God."
John 3:19

If you are a Christian, and you have had that moment of accepting Christ, you probably know and recognize all of that to be true. But let me back up a bit for those who might just be beginning in their quest for the truth.

When I was searching, I noticed that contained within the tenets of every religion known to man, the concepts of doing what is right and loving others are taught. It seems that we all inherently know that there are positive consequences for doing good and negative consequences for doing bad. These canons are universal to all people of all times. It becomes evident if we look deep enough into the doctrines of all of today's remaining religions, that they *all* have merit in their common instructions on how we should live good and holy lives so that our consequences will be those that are most desirable. So then, why is it that Christians are so insistent on the need for everyone to know the name "Jesus?" If we just have to do what is right, why is believing in Jesus so important? And why do they want us to read the Bible?

We will see clearly in later chapters the *ultimate* importance of believing in Jesus. It is as embedded in our science as the laws of physics themselves.

But for now, the importance of believing is to save your health and your well being, and to move you into the direction of life, saving you from death. It is within His name. The name "Jesus" is the same in whatever language you learn it: it always means "The Lord Saves." He saves us now, and He will ultimately save us later.

2

- Awareness -

"Wake up O sleeper, rise from the dead."
Ephesians 5:14

As I shared with you earlier, at one point I was very lost. My inner dialog was a mess. I was confused about right and wrong, I was afraid, and I was lost. At that time, although I knew that things in this world were not as they should be, I was skeptical that the answer and the truth could be found in God's word in the Bible.

Growing to truly believe in Jesus as an adult was not easy. But, I *now* know that if anyone, even an adult, actually seeks God with the openness to believe, that God will without a doubt reveal Himself and His truth to them. And, He will do it in a way that is completely personal to their needs and their unique situation. Wherever you are and with whatever it takes, if you truly seek God, He will confirm His reality and His awesome power and love to you. **"Ask and it will be given to you; seek and you will find; knock and the door will be opened to you." Matthew 7:7**

Because I was very stubborn by nature, coming to truly believe and trust in God was a lengthy process for me. I only share my story with you because God has compelled me to. I am otherwise a private person, and this information is all quite private. But as I now understand, my experiences may help to strengthen your faith. And I now know that nothing else is more important for you than to truly believe, so I have shared some of them. And I hope that you will take from them whatever resonates with you.

The Face of God 29

I was able to take the first step towards believing when I was humbled enough to truly seek God and to ask for His forgiveness. I asked to be forgiven of my self-righteousness, and also of my arrogance for thinking I could possibly know what was best. I became humbled enough to recognize that I made a horrible god. I felt much like the character in the movie *Bruce Almighty* 1, when he discovered that in a world where he answered prayers as he pleased, manipulated others, and attempted to orchestrate the world around him to suit his desires, everything became a chaotic mess very quickly.

The one true living God, however, *does* have all of the right answers, and they are right for all of us at all times as part of his intricate grander plan, where order and peace become the final result. So, having learned this same lesson, I became humbled enough to turn to Him, and I asked for the Holy Spirit to dwell in me and to guide my new life.

But I had a long way to go toward understanding all that that meant. The first concept I needed to grasp in order to lay the foundation for a true understanding of God's word, and a true belief in God's many forms, was that we really are souls living in an earthly body. And when I found myself experiencing the consequences of my actions in a place that felt like hell, one of the first things I needed to recognize in order to stop the downward spiral of events in my life was that my soul was separate from my circumstances.

The entire world could be crashing down around me, people could hate me, I could be unemployed, and I could be surrounded by debt collectors and negative doomsayers. My relationships with significant others could fall apart. My physical health could be a disaster. From all outward appearances, life could appear hopeless. And yet my soul could still be filled with love and hope. I could still be filled with joy and peace.

- Our souls are separate from our circumstances. -

At a certain point, when I had begun to believe in the messages of the Bible, I read about the "fruits of the Spirit" in Galatians. To me, it described that a body filled with the Spirit of God, rather than the spirit of its earthly circumstances, will grow to produce these fruits: love, joy, peace, patience, kindness, goodness, faithfulness, gentleness and self-control. My life at the time had none of these things.

But, in a Spirit-directed way, I decided to take each word and meditate on it. Lying in my bed, alone in what had been my misery, I started with the word "love." I asked God to fill me with His Holy Spirit so I could feel His love. I imagined being truly loved. And I focused all of my attention on the word *love*.

Slowly I began to feel love in my spirit, and my entire makeup started to change. A small smile of comfort began to develop on my face. God was filling me with love.

Then I meditated on the word "joy." I pictured swinging my children in the air and falling down, laughing with them in my arms; pure joy, really. This brought a tear of relief to my eyes (I mean this literally, since our tears contain chemicals from stress-related hormones, which crying can release).

I soaked in that moment and allowed God's Spirit to fill me with wonderful joy. Next, I allowed His Spirit to envelop me with the word "peace." And sure enough, the stress and anxiety resulting from the disasters in my physical world diminished, as I bathed in God's peace. I thought about and meditated on each of the fruits of the Spirit; and as

I felt my breathing change, my heart rate change, and my entire physical being change, I became renewed. I came away from that time feeling refreshed, with a completely different outlook on life.

Despite the fact that my circumstances were ominous, depressing and fearful, I was able to experience a different reality, one where I felt the presence of God by meditating on His words. This quiet time in His presence left me overflowing with His love and His peace, enabling me to share this joy with others I came in contact with, and allowing me to be able to better relate to others with the patience and kindness that had come directly from God's Spirit.

This experience reminded me of brainwave-activity studies that reveal how our minds perceive real physical things and imagined things similarly. For example, when we see an apple, certain areas of our brain light up with activity. And, when we simply imagine an apple, the same brainwave activity is generated. It's as if our brains are wired to respond no differently to the reality of the material world than to the reality of our mind's creation. So much so that the American Medical Association and the American Psychological Association do not endorse the use of what psychologists call "repressed memory therapy" in the treatment of alleged childhood trauma. Repressed memory therapy is a practice in which doctors attempt to use hypnotherapy to retrieve memories from early childhood. Their reasons state that "it is impossible, without corroborative evidence, to distinguish a true memory from a false one." [2]

Which one is more real? I chose to become consciously aware of the unseen that day and focused my attention on the fruits of our spiritual God.

To become aware and to recognize that there really is a soul within our physical bodies, that it does not have to be tied to our circumstances, and that at some point that soul will become completely separated from its earthly burdens, was for me step one in my journey to true faith in God and in the power of His word.

You may have read about or seen the movie based on a well-known experiment conducted by Dr. Duncan MacDougall in 1997. 3 After weighing individuals at the moment of death and discovering the bodies weighed three-fourths of an ounce (or about 21 grams) less than before, he theorized that difference to have been the weight of the soul as it left the body.

But what is a soul? I needed to know these kinds of things. My scientific mind was not going to allow me to truly believe in God's Word as it is given in the Bible unless it made sense and corresponded with everything we have learned about the universe through science.

And, thankfully, since He created me, God knew this about me personally, so He patiently revealed to me that His Word does *not* contradict science. He further took the time to show me how His amazing work and His astounding creation, as it is explained to us through His Word in the Bible, exactly corresponds with everything our scientific research has shown us.

Not many people view the Bible in a scientific context. But as I see it now, everything we are learning about the world through our increasingly advanced science experiments is simply confirming what God's word in the bible has always said. God *is* the author of science as He created the universe, and we are getting to figure that out.

So with my "psychologist hat" on, I began to ask: What is a soul? According to *Psychology and You*, it is not easy to define. We can't touch it, find it, or pick it up. It is simply a construct.

"A construct is what scientists call a belief in something that cannot be seen or touched, but that according to evidence, actually is present."[4] We will talk more about this later. Just know that it is there. Like an observer within the walls of our bodies, our soul is there.

"Spirits" and "souls" are different things. Each human has a soul which will live on after physical death. The spirit, on the other hand, is like a driving force, a motivation that makes people behave in one way or another. For example: a group of people working together to reach the same goal are working in unity, or in the same spirit.

The level of alertness or awareness our soul has to the physical and spiritual world around us can be called our *consciousness*. We have various levels of consciousness, and throughout any given day we continuously change from one state to another. We need to grasp these concepts so we can build the frame of reference necessary for understanding the more spiritual concepts that we will be discussing later. If you already know these next truths about our minds and bodies, please bear with me. This will just serve as a reminder.

Our brains receive and process billions of bits of information every single second, yet we are only made consciously aware of a few thousand of them. [5]

How does your heart know to beat without our conscious concentration on it? How do your white blood cells know to surround a foreign object? How is it we can wake up at generally the same time every day without the aid of an alarm clock?

Obviously there are subconscious bodily functions being ordered and directed by different parts of our brains all day long that our conscious minds are not aware of. According to the doctrine of psychoanalysis founded by Sigmund Freud, *everything* we do or say – all of our behaviors – are a result of subconscious mental activity guiding our actions. In fact, the majority of what we do, and what goes on within our bodies, is controlled by the predetermined duties of cells encrypted in our DNA that we never even stop to think about. The complex workings inside of our cells – functioning throughout all of our organs in perfect coordination throughout all of our systems – are astounding. Mechanisms within our bodies are constantly monitoring our internal and external environments and sending electric signals to the necessary organs, glands, and areas of our brains to keep us in a constant state of homeostasis.

Although our brains are receiving and perceiving different forms of energy as they pass through our senses all day long, it is only when they are brought to the attention of our "minds" that we actually become aware of what is being perceived.

In grammar school we learn about the five major senses our bodies utilize to process information that is ultimately sent to the brain: *Vision* processes light waves from the environment, which go through a lens in the eye and hit the retina; *Hearing* processes sound waves to stimulate the eardrum, where hair cells are tuned to receive the information; Our sense of *touch* responds to three basic types of stimulation: physical changes, temperature and injury; Our ability to *smell* comes from olfactory bulbs that receive information from tiny hairs in the nose; *Taste* receptors respond to sweet, sour, bitter and salt. [6]

Most significant to note, however, is whether we consider any of this information coming in to be important enough to be brought out from our subconscious awareness of it and up to our frontal lobes, where thinking and understanding take place.

This concept of our brains controlling what is brought to our attention based on what we have previously deemed as important – recognized by psychologists as being controlled by our "Reticular Activating System," or RAS – is the key to our ability of becoming truly aware and enlightened as to what is taking place from a greater perspective. A person could walk around their entire life "asleep" and unaware of so much information that their brain has taken in because what they have been led to believe is important is all that they focus on. Like the aliens visiting our planet would notice, our attention stays on the things we deem relevant to reaching our earthly goals. In the meantime, what is really important would remain unrecognized.

As we are always surrounded by and bombarded with streams of information coming through our senses every day, what we have deemed most important is what our minds will recognize and actually perceive. The rest of our surroundings remain present, but unnoticed. Let's say you decide you need a new car, for example. This becomes an important decision for you. Suddenly you will notice billboard ads and television commercials for cars are everywhere. The reality is that they were always around before, but as you decided this information was now important, your Reticular

Activating System worked with you to make you more alert to their presence.

This is the psychology at work in the "law of attraction," made popular by the book called *The Secret*. This "law," stating that you will attract what you think about, can be explained by the fact that all things are present, but if your mind is focused on a goal, your RAS will make you alert to the opportunities that exist around you for achieving that goal. The truth is, all possibilities are always there, we just see the ones we have directed ourselves to see, based on what we have deemed to be important, or what we "treasure," so to speak.

"For where your treasure is, there your heart will be also."   Matthew 6:19

"Furthermore, since they did not think it worthwhile (important) **to retain the knowledge of God, he gave them over to a depraved mind..."**
Romans 1:28

If we look even deeper, we can see how our level of awareness about what is going on within and without our bodies throughout the day, and throughout our life, is also determined on a cellular level by electrical and chemical activity in our brains. When we sleep, we can see this activity decrease. When we are awake, the activity is greatly increased. During times when we are as alert as we can possibly be, the amount of sodium and potassium ions (electrically charged particles) being traded by our brain cells as they spark activity and share "information" is astounding. Yet again, only the smallest fraction of this activity begets the form of a thought.

Today, many psychologists recognize the possibility of other senses at work within our systems as well. The existence of extra sensory perception, or ESP, is more readily accepted in science now than when it was first introduced. But as a culture we find it hard to believe in things we cannot see.

At one time most people believed the radio would never work. Then, the television was impossible. Moving images traveling through the air in your room! Now we have cell phones and wireless Internet service. Trillions of bits of information passing through our atmosphere, none of which we can see, and yet it is all "real." [7] We have only scratched the surface of the limitless possibilities for other unseen phenomena. It is all around us at all times.

In an experiment by Youtz, in 1968, we learned that some people develop stronger abilities to sense extraordinary things than others. For example, a few people are so sensitive that they can tell a difference in an object's color by using only touch. [8]

Some evolutionists, who have studied the changes in the human brain, believe that our species may have once utilized a whole host of other senses, like those seen in bats or praying mantises. But, as we evolved, these scientists speculate that our physical bodies developed what proved to be more useful senses for our survival. And, as other senses fell into disuse, they atrophied and ceased to exist. [9]

There is apparently only so much room within the walls of our skulls to house our brains, leading to selective trimming of excess, unneeded space. However, when we look at the portions of the brain that we know through science are designated for different functions, there still seems to be so much brain matter that exists whose function has not been clearly identified.

If real estate within our skull is so valuable that only the most needed portions of the brain have been allowed to remain through its evolution, then some important use must exist for the remaining unidentified areas.

Some scientists speculate that unusual or extraordinary senses once used are still in place but are just dormant. In the same way exercising a muscle makes it grow stronger, it is speculated these extra senses could be strengthened again if they were exercised. Others speculate that maybe these unmarked areas of the brain *are* being used, but just in ways we cannot detect yet.

As reported in *Psychology and You*, "it is important to note that scientists, researchers, and others who study how our bodies work know almost nothing in comparison to the vast intelligence of our universe." [10]

In other words, there is so much we don't know about and we cannot see. The universe is full of wonders and constructs we don't even know exist. Only the spiritual, ever-present God knows and sees it all.

"Therefore once more I will astound these people with wonder upon wonder, the wisdom of the wise will perish, and the intelligence of the intelligent will vanish."
Isaiah 29:14

The truth is there are more so-called realities in the universe that we *cannot* see than ones we can. And what we inevitably do see in the universe once existed in a form we were unable to see. We will discuss this in more detail later.

For now, take note of the wave spectrum of light energy. We have learned that light energy exists in a spectrum, and that our physical eyes have the ability to take in only a small portion of that spectrum.

But the reality is that light also exists in energy wavelengths that our eyes have not been created to see. The same goes for sound waves. As we know, dogs can hear the sound of a dog whistle that humans can't because we are only designed to "hear" a small portion of a larger spectrum of sound waves. Radio waves, electromagnetic waves, etc., the examples are everywhere. Once again, what we see, hear, or consciously perceive is only the tiniest portion of what exists.

God separated the light from the darkness, as we read in the beginning of Genesis. Now scientists tell us that the entire universe is made up of two types of matter: light matter, which can absorb and reflect light; and dark matter, which cannot (making it unable for our eyes to "see").

The Milky Way Galaxy is actually said to have 10 times more dark matter than matter we can see. And as much as 99% of the mass of the entire universe has been estimated to be dark matter. [11]

Only a small fraction of the energy of the universe has manifested itself in the form of atoms which we can "see" as the building block of light matter. But the rest of the energy is still there. It just hasn't been spoken into its recognizable particle state yet. (More about that later…)

Okay, I hope I haven't lost anyone. Maybe all of that was just a review, or maybe it was new information for you. In any case, I had to get it all out there to lay the foundation for the next chapters. The point of it all was that even the most brilliant of minds on our planet are unable to understand and to be aware of all things. We are limited by our humanity. And, for the most part, we focus only on what we can see. But, as a whole, it seems we are becoming more and more aware of the importance of "unseen" realities. Once again, God is calling us. He is waking up our subconscious awareness and slowly bringing it into the light.

Common themes in our conscious thoughts as human beings that uncover the unseen universe around us have been emerging in awakened individuals all over our little planet. In our modern world you can often get a feel for the pervasive thoughts of the majority by looking at the best-selling books of the time.

Lately, in books such as *The Secret, The Power of Intentions, The Seven Habits of Highly Effective People,* and many others, our awareness of the power we have to change the physical world around us by making changes from within is blossoming. This construct is something I too was fortunately awakened to notice. But beyond that, God has shown me that His plan, which will be changing the entire physical world as we know it, is so much more than any of these books suggest. And that what is *really* important is something that none of these books address.

"And do this, understanding the present time: The hour has come for you to wake up from your slumber, because our salvation is nearer now than when we first believed. The night is nearly over; the day is almost here."
Romans 13:11

"So we fix our eyes not on what is seen, but on what is unseen. For what is seen is temporary, but what is unseen is eternal."
2 Corinthians 4:18

3

- Thoughts -

(Almost) every thought you have and every action you take is merely a result of current and past influences of other people's thoughts and actions around you.

Continuing in my faith, and continuing to grow in my understanding of God's word, meant that I would need to understand more about what was going on within and around us that we can't see, so that the scripture I was beginning to read more often would make sense.

Recent developments in our scientific understanding of thoughts have aided me in my understanding of God's words tremendously. And it seems as though more and more of us are recognizing the power of our thoughts just as Jesus and his disciples were trying to explain 2,000 years ago.

Scientists are now able to demonstrate that every time you release a thought in your mind, your body manufactures and dumps chemicals into your bloodstream. The types of chemicals released depend on the thought produced. For example, thoughts of a sleepy or sad nature create melatonin and other depressant chemicals. Thoughts of joyful moments produce serotonin and other stimulating chemicals. Thoughts of sex produce hormones full of yet another set of chemicals. It is important to understand that the cells throughout our body actually feed on these chemicals. [1]

Picture an antacid tablet being dropped into a glass of water. It dissolves until the water is chalky and every molecule of water appears saturated with this substance. In the same way, when our brains release these chemicals, they saturate the blood and the fluids that comprise our bodies, until every cell within us becomes covered with these chemicals.

Scientists now observe that our cells actually develop openings for the specific chemicals they are coming into contact with. The peptides – long molecules of linked amino acids – in the various chemicals are of varying shapes. So, our cells will transform themselves to create more openings that fit the shape of the peptides in the chemicals surrounding the cells. [2]

It follows that if you release one type of thought – a sad thought, for example – the cells in your body will feed on its chemical energy and will, in a sense, "crave" it again to fill the holes, or openings, that they have specifically developed for it. Then, you will likely be led to produce another thought of the same type to experience another release of those same chemicals.

In the same way drug users require more of the same drug to satisfy their chemical cravings, you will subconsciously crave more and more of those negative thoughts to feed the chemical craving of your own cells. [3] Hence, those negative, sad thoughts can lead to a chemical depression.

The same would be true for all kinds of emotions, including anger, resentment, jealousy, revenge, and thoughts of lack and worry, just to name a few. These thoughts invariably lead us to acts that would in turn create more negative feelings, leaving our cells open and craving for more and more of this cyclical, negative chemical rush. In the same way we become chemically dependent and addicted to drugs, our bodies also become chemically addicted to the chemicals released by our thoughts.

"As for you, you were dead in your transgressions and sins, in which you used to live when you followed the ways of this world and of the ruler of the kingdom of the air, the spirit who is now at work in those who are disobedient. All of us also lived among them at one time, *gratifying the cravings of our sinful nature and following its desires and thoughts.* **Like the rest, we were by nature objects of wrath.**
But because of his great love for us, God, who is rich in mercy, made us alive with Christ even when we were dead in transgressions – and it is by grace you have been saved."
Ephesians 2:1-5

Just as we can now see the negative effects from thoughts that come from a sad, bad, or otherwise sinful nature, we can also see positive effects on our lives stemming from thoughts that are from God.

A few years ago, I heard of a study that showed that every time a person does a good deed for another, their brain produces (or signals for the production of) serotonin in their body. Further, even when an observer sees a person doing a good deed for another, their brain also signals for the production of serotonin. 4

Serotonin, not surprisingly, is the main ingredient in most pharmaceutical drugs being prescribed to treat depression. When released in our bodies, serotonin has an anti-depressant, feel-good effect on us.

Other studies point to the amazing effects of the chemical oxytocin, which is released with thoughts of a loved one, or in pleasurable activities. Oxytocin plays a huge role in bonding.

Studies have shown that blocking the activity of oxytocin in rats or sheep causes mothers to reject their young. And on the flip side, injecting virgin female rats with oxytocin causes them to adopt other rats' pups as their own.

This chemical also is thought to be important in the formation of pair bonds (the scientific name for monogamous couples). In humans, the release can be stimulated by sex or simply by physical contact with a loved one, and it has a powerful, relaxing effect.

Further studies in animals called prairie voles, known for living out their lives in monogamous pairs, showed that blocking the effects of oxytocin prevented them from forming into monogamous couples. Imagine this chemical at work within the bodies of healthy families, how it keeps couples together and keeps parents involved and connected with their children. [5]

Other experiments have suggested that the amount of oxytocin in our system may determine our ability to trust. In one study, subjects who inhaled oxytocin in a nasal spray were more likely to hand over cash to strangers, knowing that they might not get it back. [6]

These are all great studies. It is truly amazing that we have the power to create and release these chemicals just by our thoughts! As we saw earlier, our brains cannot tell the difference between the physical reality and the one only our minds can see.

Remember the way the brain activity was exactly the same with a real and an imagined apple? The same physiological responses result.

What if we could live every day, bathed in thoughts of gratitude and love? We could be filling ourselves with oxytocin and serotonin. With their effects, we would be more apt to help and give to others in need, which would in turn release more serotonin within us, which would create a whole cycle of improved health and wellness.

We will discuss more of this later; but as just a thought for now, I am guessing that the Good Samaritan that God calls us to be, and those who are able to live by God's greatest command to love Him and to love others as you love yourself, are those who are filled with these chemicals. These individuals must be aware of the truth of God's sovereignty. With the knowledge that we can trust God to replace anything we give away, then we can, without worry, freely give to others, and trust that God will continue to supply us with all that we need.

"Therefore I tell you, do not worry about your life, what you will eat; or about your body, what you will wear. Life is more than food, and the body more than clothes. Consider the ravens: They do not sow or reap; they have no storeroom or barn. Yet God feeds them. And how much more valuable you are than birds. Who of you by worrying can add a single hour to his life? Since you cannot do this very thing, why do you worry about the rest?"
Luke 12:22

"Never will I leave you; never will I forsake you."
Hebrews 13:5

But who could possibly think these thoughts all day as we are surrounded by this real and difficult world? The answer to this, (if you haven't already guessed), is coming.

"For my thoughts are not your thoughts, neither are your ways my ways, declares the Lord. As the heavens are higher than the earth, so are my ways higher than your ways and my thoughts than your thoughts."
Isaiah 55:8

It now seems clear that the thoughts we ponder can make us sick or make us well as they affect our bodies from within. What is also very important to know is that they also affect what is around us.

Another study really opened my eyes to the power of thoughts. It was a study on water conducted by a Japanese researcher named Dr. Masaru Emoto. What his experiment revealed indicated the power of our thoughts over things outside our bodies.

But, before I share his amazing experiment, let me start with another experiment I learned about in college. This was a study on twins that, to me, revealed the phenomenon that our thoughts escape our own skin, literally going out into the universe.

Although our skin seems like a barrier, when you look at it more closely, on many levels it is really no barrier at all. Our skin is made up of cells that are made up of molecules, which are simply combinations of atoms.

Atoms are mostly just empty space, spattered with energy particles, called protons and electrons – little bits of positive and negative energy forces. You may have learned about what we once thought was the "dense" nucleus of an atom. But, as scientists have shown us, even the nucleus is mostly just space spattered with protons and neutrons.

Quantum scientists have shown us that even those tiny bits of positive and negative energized particles called protons and neutrons and electrons are themselves mostly just space made up of even smaller quantum particles. And scientists say that these quantum particles themselves can hardly be considered solid things at all.

Through the work of Max Planck, Albert Einstein, Louis de Broglie, Arthur Compton, Niels Bohr and many others, current scientific theory holds that *all* particles *also* have a wave nature (and vice versa.) [7] These tiny quantum particles, that together form the protons, neutrons, and electrons that make up every atom in every molecule of every substance in the universe, are actually said to be not just particles, but more like waves of energy that seem to come and go, in and out of existence.

It is a bit mind-boggling to actually picture, but this concept has become more clearly understood. It has been referred to as the *illusion of solidity*. The reason macroscopic objects appear to be stable and occupy a constant volume can be explained by what is called the Pauli Exclusion Principle. In summary, it basically explains that the electrons within each atom must revolve around the nucleus in different energy level orbits with a repulsive property keeping them from occupying the same orbital plane, essentially keeping the atoms from being squeezed together. The magnetic forces of repulsion from within the atom and electrostatic forces from outside the atoms keep these particles (which themselves are made up of quantum particles that exists in waves of energy) from being compacted together. Without these forces, all of the atoms that make up the macroscopic object would collapse and occupy a much smaller volume, if any. But for now, with the forces at work on all of the electrons in motion throughout our bodies, even we are a part of the illusion of solidity.

With all this in mind, we can imagine what happens in our bodies when waves of chemical energy are produced that are based on our thoughts; of course they travel through the space that makes up our physical body and then out into the space that is beyond our outer layer of skin cells.

How could our porous skin confine that energy? It can't, in the same way it can't keep any other types of energy out. If you are exposed to radioactive energy for example, we know your cells will be greatly affected. With some touch screen technology we can actually see how the electromagnetic waves emanating from our fingers can be detected.

You may wonder: Will the chemicals from the thoughts of others around you affect your cells? Yes. Other types of energy will as well.

All of the known macroscopic objects of the entire universe are made up of the same 118 known elements, simply combined in different forms to create all things – including us. These elements are all made up of molecules, which are made up of atoms, which are made up of protons, then neutrons and electrons. Further, as we now know, these particles are themselves made up of even smaller quantum particles – quarks and such, which can be seen existing as waves of energy. It is this energy that is throughout the makeup of every atom of every cell of every element that makes up all things – again including us. Without barriers, to keep this energy in or out, we are all connected to each other and to all forms of things that make up our entire universe.

"Be completely humble and gentle; be patient, bearing with one another in love. Make every effort to keep the *unity* of the Spirit through the bond of peace. There is one body and one Spirit -- just as you were called to one hope when you were called -- one Lord, one faith, one baptism; one God and Father of all, who is over all and through all and in all."
Ephesians 4:2

As we will also see later, those who have been able to believe in God, and whose cells have been cleansed and transformed by the washing of the Holy Spirit, and whose minds are set on Christ, are especially connected. They become filled with the same energy frequency, so to speak.

"Finally, brothers, goodbye. Aim for perfection, listen to my appeal, be of *one* mind, live in peace. And the God of love and peace will be with you."
2 Corinthians 13:11

During the last few decades, scientists have used sensitive measuring devices to detect the electrical impulses created by brain activity. These devices have been able to pick up this energy three or four inches from the skull. [8] With more advanced machines, we could probably detect the energy at even greater distances.

In the twin study I mentioned, scientists took sets of twins at different ages and looked for the possibility of mental telepathy or extra sensory perception (ESP). They wanted to see if the twins had the ability to sense the thoughts of each other.

The twins were divided by a partition. On one side one child was asked to look at a picture of one of three objects and to think about that object: a ball, a chair or a cat, for example. The other twin was asked which of the three objects was being observed by his partner. By sheer chance, the twin had a 33.3 percent chance of guessing correctly. In the youngest of ages the response astonished the experimenters by resulting in as much as 55 percent correct answers.

As the children aged, their percentage of correct answers slowly decreased until, at a certain age, they were at 33 percent: the probability for guessing one out of three. 9

What does this mean?

It could mean many things. One possibility is that telepathy does indeed exist. This ability may be amplified in twins who share the same DNA and who shared the same environment in the womb.

But it is not limited to twins or even siblings. If this ability of extra sensory perception exists, it stands to reason that it could become stronger among anyone who makes an effort to use it and develop it.

Also, this study seems to indicate that as we age, we develop some sort of ability for obscuring our thoughts. Some call it a defense mechanism.

As children, we are open and unashamed, innocent, and without need of barriers to keep our unwholesome thoughts to ourselves.

But as we grow and become corrupted by the thoughts of the world, we learn the negative consequences of acting on bad thoughts and we develop a defense mechanism that keeps our selfish or inappropriate worldly thoughts from escaping.

On the flip side, we also learn not to sense the chemical thoughts of others. As children, without a sense of judgment, we are much more open to recognizing them. So, without the need of barriers to keep unwholesome thoughts to ourselves, nor the wall of judgment to keep the energy from the thoughts of others out, we, as children, appear to be more open and connected to the flow of energy generated by thoughts.

These suggestions have probably only scratched the surface of what is going on within as we age and change over time, from being open and believing children to becoming closed and unbelieving adults. It is important to note, however, that Jesus repeatedly talked of the need to be open and to believe again in order to receive the "kingdom of heaven."

"I tell you the truth, unless you change and become like little children, you will never enter the kingdom of heaven. Therefore, whoever humbles himself like this child is the greatest in the kingdom of heaven."
Matthew 18:2

As we can witness, children have this amazing ability to believe. Whatever their parents tell them, they can believe with all their hearts. Santa Claus, the Easter Bunny – they don't question these things. They don't doubt, until sadly, with age, that precious, wide-eyed belief turns into skepticism mixed with the need for physical proof in order to believe.

Yet, over and over, scripture tells us we have to truly believe without being able to see first. It's called having faith – believing in something we cannot physically see. We were not around to witness the miracles of Christ. We cannot actually see what He did for us when He sacrificed himself on the cross in atonement for our sins. But we are called to believe in it. With the true open faith of a child, we can choose to believe in the word of God. And, as we will see, it is by this faith that we are saved.

"But when he asks, he must believe and not doubt, because he who doubts is like a wave of the sea, blown and tossed by the wind."
James 1:6

"I tell you the truth: Anyone who will not receive the kingdom of God like a little child will never enter it."
Mark 10:15

It is clear from scripture that to not miss out on what is really important, we have to humble ourselves as adults. We have to stop thinking we know everything and accept, just like a child would, that there are wonderful things taking place all around us that we cannot physically see, but that by faith, as silly as it seems, are there for us to just believe.

"See that you do not look down on one of these little ones. For I tell you that their angels in heaven always see the face of my Father in heaven."
Matthew 18:10

I will never forget what my daughter said to me about her memory of heaven just as she turned three. At that time, I was not a believer in God. I had never taken her to church or even offered any information on the subject to her. This came out of nowhere.

I used to lie in bed with her each evening, reading and chatting with her before saying goodnight. One night, with a sigh, she said to me, "Mommy, I miss heaven."

I thought: *What? How does she know heaven?*

The Face of God 53

I became curious. I thought that maybe she could teach me something.

So I asked her, "You remember heaven? What do you remember about it?"

She sweetly said, "God was there, and he was *sooo* nice."

Now I was really curious. I wanted to know more.

"Like, what did he do?" I asked.

"He gave me everything I wanted," she said in the most longing yet peaceful tone.

I was amazed that she remembered the feeling of having all of her needs met, of complete love, of wholeness. I tried prodding her further.

"What kinds of things did he give you?" I asked.

Here is where the communication broke down for this precious three year old, who didn't know the words to describe those feelings or even what those "things" were.

So, she answered, "Um, I think like jewelry and stuff?"

How can a three year old possibly know how to describe the treasures in heaven? The closest, most precious earthly thing she could name that might resemble the value of what God had provided was jewelry.

Today, I am reminded of how impossible it is for our minds to imagine what God has in store for us. Jesus had to describe the kingdom of heaven using things we could envision, like seeds and gardens. To take a spiritual concept and try to explain it with a material representation so our earthly minds could fathom it must have been a difficult translation for Jesus. It would be like explaining the concept of hedge funds to a four year old who just knows that money comes in coins and is shiny. Behind the scenes of our young, naïve, earthly eyes, so much spiritual activity is underway.

"Then Jesus asked, "What is the kingdom of God like? What shall I compare it to? It is like a mustard seed, which a man took and planted in his garden. It grew and became a tree, and the birds of the air perched in its branches."
Luke 13:18

And Jesus patiently taught…

"Do not store up for yourselves treasures on earth, where moth and rust destroy, and where thieves break in and steal. But store up for yourselves treasures in heaven, where moth and rust do not destroy, and where thieves do not break in and steal. For where your treasure is, there your heart will be also."
Matthew 6:19

Not only does Jesus explain the concept of the everlasting treasures of heaven, as my daughter had somehow experienced, He also explains to us that where our hearts, minds and thoughts are, *there we will also be.* As explained by the Reticular Activating System I referenced earlier, we will achieve the goal that we are alert and open to recognizing. If what we deem to be important are temporary earthly treasures, then that is what our attention will stay focused on and where we will remain. But knowing now that what lies in heaven is far more important, and has lasting, eternal value, our goals should be focused there instead. And by focusing on heaven, heaven is what we will "attract," and heaven is where we will eventually be.

But, I may be getting a little ahead of myself. Let's get back to our discussion on thoughts.

As we can now see through scientific research, our thoughts are laced with chemicals that are made up of smaller particles, which in turn simply consist of waves of energy. This energy affects not only our bodies but also the world around us.

This next study, to me, made this even more evident.

Dr. Masaru Emoto discovered that thoughts, words, and music all have a physical affect on water. Using a technique he developed with a very powerful microscope and high speed photography in a very cold lab, he was able to capture photographs of the newly formed crystals of frozen water samples. What the photos revealed was astounding. Water samples that had positive thoughts and loving words directed toward them revealed crystal formations that appeared like beautifully organized, colorful snowflakes. While water samples exposed to harsh music and negative words and thoughts crystallized in dull, asymmetric, unorganized ways. When we consider how much of the earth is covered in water, we can imagine what our thoughts are doing to affect our planet.

And when we consider how much of our bodies are made up of water, we can imagine the direct affect of our thoughts on our every cell. 10

It was on the same day that I read about this study that God also led me to his word in Philippians for the first time.

"Finally brothers, whatever is true, whatever is noble, whatever is right, whatever is pure, whatever is lovely, whatever is admirable -- if anything is excellent or praiseworthy -- *think* about such things. Whatever you

have learned or received or heard from me, or seen in me- put it into practice. And the God of peace will be with you."
Philippians 4:8

Knowing this study was the kind of "evidence" I would need to believe God's word was true, He showed both that scripture and that study to me at the same time so I could make that connection. Reading more of His word, it became clear that He repeatedly tells us to count our blessings, to think positive thoughts, and to be full of gratitude in all things. And hundreds of times we are told to love. As science shows us, what we have been told to do in the Bible is actually the healthiest way for us to live.

As Rick Warren says in his book *The Purpose Driven Life,* God revealed this thousands of years before psychologists understood it: "Be careful how you think; your life is shaped by your thoughts." 11

Our Creator designed us to live healthy and well and gave us the best instructions on how to do so. And, as we will see, He also has provided us with the means to be able to follow His instructions.

"Be joyful always; pray continually; give thanks in all circumstances, for this is God's will for you in Christ Jesus."
1 Thessalonians 5:16

"Let no debt remain outstanding except the continuing debt to love one another, for he who loves his fellow man has fulfilled all the law. The commandments, 'Do not commit adultery,' 'Do not murder,' 'Do not steal,' 'Do not covet,' and whatever other

commandments there may be, are summed up in this one rule: Love your neighbor as yourself. Love does no harm to its neighbor. Therefore, love is the fulfillment of the law.

Rejoice in the Lord always. I will say it again: Rejoice. Let your gentleness be evident to all. The Lord is near. Do not be anxious about anything, but in everything, by prayer and petition, with thanksgiving, present your requests to God. And the peace of God, which transcends all understanding, will guard your hearts and your minds in Christ Jesus.

Philippians 4:4

Up until the early part of the twentieth century, something called *embryonic education* was taught in Japan. Their belief was that the voices, thoughts, and feelings of the parents, grandparents, and other family members influenced the development of the fetus, which, as we should note, is surrounded by water, or embryonic fluid, in the womb. 12

Centuries later, we are now able to see this to be true. We have made huge strides in modern medicine, and with amazing technology we have been able to witness many of the marvelous, invisible to the naked eye, workings of our bodies.

But what science is able to prove to be true today was already believed to be true centuries ago. This applies just as much to people who lived millenniums ago. On faith they followed God's commands and were prospered, healed, and even brought back to life by so believing.

God loves us, and His instructions and commands for us in the Bible are actually for our physical well-being as well as our spiritual life.

Imagine if we all believed and followed God's instructions in the Bible. We would produce so much serotonin in our bodies by thinking positive thoughts, doing good deeds for our neighbors, and loving others that the number of cases of chemically induced depression would disappear.

Not surprisingly, the National Institute of Mental Health reports that "Research over the past two decades has shown ... that depression is an important risk factor for heart disease along with high blood cholesterol and high blood pressure." - *National Institute of Mental Health.* 13

Thankfully, by the design of our Creator, serotonin is released when we think of loved ones and feel grateful. And serotonin is produced by following God's commands; not only to think these thoughts but to act on them by loving one another.

Science shows us that in addition to lifting our moods, this chemical also inhibits adrenaline, boosts the immune system, and lowers cholesterol, again helping to prevent heart attacks, strokes, and many other types of physical illnesses. 14

Not only has God given us the means to produce serotonin and oxytocin, as we learned about earlier, but we can also add endorphins to the mix.

Endorphins in the average person are heavily concentrated in the part of the brain that brings us pleasure (Romagnano & Hamill, 1984). They contribute to a feeling of well-being and help block pain. The reverse is also true. If we inject a chemical that stops the operation of endorphins, the person feels fatigued and gets depressed. But, when someone thinks positively and relaxes, this increases the level of endorphins in the body (Levine & Gordon, 1985).

This is obviously not a complete list of every chemical that is involved in our body chemistry; we have only named a few. But hopefully you see the point – that all of these chemicals can be released according to our thoughts. And that not coincidentally, God's word tells us repeatedly to think positively, not to worry, and to act out of love. He instructs us to think this way for many reasons, including His desire to bring us back to the place of perfect health – no more depression, stress, worries, and anxiety: all known now to be root causes of physical illnesses that can lead to death. God's plan for a new earth is one where there is no more death. In the book of Revelations we see the vision of the prophet, who saw the new heaven and the new Earth,

"Now the dwelling of God is with men, and he will live with them. They will be his people, and God himself will be with them and be their God. He will wipe every tear from their eyes. There will be no more death or mourning or crying or pain, for the old order of things has passed away."
Revelation 21:3

Our thoughts affect our bodies in a physical sense to such a great extent that a group of prominent medical doctors have recently put together a book called *The Handbook on Religion and Health.* In it we are shown the positive effects of our beliefs (our thoughts) and our faith on everything from asthma to yeast infections. [15] Thoughts of God and faith in His word can literally make us well.

I would venture to say, however, that most of us, including me, allow our thoughts to be of the world, causing us to obsess over material things, worries, fears, anxieties, work, and others' opinions to the point that we find our minds coveting the things of the earth that will one day cease to exist.

In speaking of that day, Jesus warns us: **"Be careful or your hearts will be weighed down with dissipation, drunkenness and the anxieties of life, and that day will close on you unexpectedly like a trap." Luke 21:34**

We are repeatedly told in the Bible not to worry or even entertain troubling thoughts. Imagine all of the chemicals associated with fear and anxiety that we have been feeding our cells. Jesus again tells us how we should think thoughts of gratitude instead, and he made it especially clear that we should do this when we are consuming food and drink. The science underlying this instruction is just now being revealed, as we will see in later chapters. For now, just note that the consumption of food should always be paired with thoughts of Christ and gratitude for what He has done for us.

As He broke the bread and prepared to serve it to his disciples, Jesus said: **"This is my body, which is for you; do this in remembrance of me. This cup is the new covenant in my blood; do this, whenever you drink it, in remembrance of me." 1 Corinthians 11:24**

Then the apostle Paul explains: **"For anyone who eats and drinks without recognizing the body of the Lord eats and drinks judgment on himself. That is why many among you are weak and sick, and a number of you have fallen asleep." 1 Corinthians 11:2**

After seeing what happened to the water in Dr. Emoto's study, one can begin to imagine what might be happening to the chemical and molecular structure of our food and drink as we think these thoughts while we digest the food and drink into our bodies. Again, we will talk more of this later.

For now:

"Do not conform any longer to the pattern of this world, but be transformed by the renewing of your mind."
Romans 12:2

"Therefore I tell you, do not worry about your life..."
Matthew 6:25

"I would like you to be free from concern."
1 Corinthians 7:32

"Since then, you have been raised with Christ, set your hearts on things above, where Christ is seated at the right hand of God. Set your minds on things above, not earthly things."
Colossians 3:1

"We demolish arguments and every pretension that sets itself up against the knowledge of God, and we take captive every thought to make it obedient to Christ."
2 Corinthians 10:3

If only I could recognize every thought that presents itself and make it "obedient to Christ" before it settles in and stirs up my emotions, things would be much easier.

Unfortunately, I don't always catch my negative thoughts in time. Sometimes I hear something someone else has said, or I witness someone else doing something, and I am not even consciously aware of the thoughts I had about it that led to the emotions that were released. I have to force myself to think back on what was said or done to recognize why the chemicals that are lingering in my system are even present in the fist place. Such thoughts occur so subconsciously.

As we read this scripture again we can see that it is not only our thoughts that need to be considered, but also the "pretensions" that "set themselves up"…

"We demolish arguments and every pretension that sets itself up against the knowledge of God, and we take captive every thought to make it obedient to Christ." 2 Corinthians 10:3

So what is a "pretension?"

The prefix *pre* usually means "before," and "tension" shares the same root word for tendency – or "a natural or prevailing disposition to move, proceed, or act in some direction or toward some point, end, or result." 16

I wonder if anyone caught this. This definition states that the end result is already in mind, *pre*determining how or which way we move. Or another way to think of it is that our *pre*existing goals held subconsciously in the back of our minds determine our choices and guide our actions, just as we talked about earlier when our RAS signals us to become aware of what we previously deemed important for achieving our end goal.

There isn't anything in God's creation that wasn't made complete with both the beginning and the end in mind.

He gave us every living plant that within themselves contained the seeds in their fruit to bear them life again after death. He created the chicken with the egg already within its design (neither came first – they were created at the same time). The beginning and the end were created together. This is why your pretensions have within them the end result in mind. And along those same lines, for whomever needs to remember this: There was never a fall without a redemption already created.

I am the Alpha and the Omega... Revelations 1:8 (The beginning and the end.)

With the end of your life and your final destination already known to God and therefore also known by His Spirit that is living within you, you were led to read this book as a pretension to your final destination; (just as another example.)

But, are you able to recognize when you are being driven by fear? Fear has become for many, a driving force; fear and control, (or the need to feel in control and the fear of not being able to control.) Much of what we do or say unfortunately comes from a place of fear. And yet it doesn't have to. We look into this further later, but as we will see, *all* of our fears are based on lies against the truth of God. They are pretensions that set themselves up against the knowledge of God.

The knowledge of God – we need to *know* that He is sovereign, He is in control and He loves us. We therefore have nothing to fear. All of our needs will be met. We are free to act on love, not fear.

To stop those pretensions in their tracks, the word of God is our greatest weapon. We will talk much more about this later. But for now, remember when Jesus was tempted in the desert, even He used the word of God to correct each falsehood thrown at Him by the devil. He used the words of God to prevent any words of the devil from taking root.

"No weapon forged against you shall prevail."
Isaiah 54:17

Instead, God's word and His Holy Spirit gives us hope.

"May the God of hope fill you with all joy and peace as you trust in him, so that you may overflow with hope by the power of the Holy Spirit."
Romans 15:13

Getting back to our discussion, in the past few years studies of eye movement and brainwave activity during decision-making tests have suggested that our decisions are actually made for us several seconds before we are consciously aware of them. Researchers were able to see the decisions being made according to brain activity several seconds before the subjects determined that they had even made a decision! [17]

Does anyone else wonder, then, what it is inside of us making the decision for us, if it is made even before we are consciously aware of it?

Again, in psychoanalysis Freud explained that every decision we make and the behavior that results from it is, in turn, a result of subconscious desires and motivations or intentions (what the scripture called "pretensions").

So, if we are led to make decisions and behave one way or another by our subconscious intentions, where do our subconscious intentions come from? As we saw earlier, they are aligned with our end goals and what we deem important. And our end goals, or what we deem important, come from our thoughts that shape our beliefs about the world.

But we just learned that our thoughts come from our subconscious pretensions – that are shaped by our thoughts! If this all sounds like a vicious cycle, that's because it is!

Everything is a cycle: the chicken bears the egg that hatches the chicken; the trees grow the fruit that bears the seed that grows the tree... it's all cyclical – our mental processes included. Psychologists often refer to the cycle of our decision making process as "loop feedback." We will talk more about this in the next chapter.

For now, just note that scripture says:

"From within, out of men's hearts come evil thoughts... Nothing outside a man can make him unclean." (Mark 7)

"The real problem is in the hearts and minds of men. It is easier to denature plutonium than to denature the evil spirit of man." - Albert Einstein

4
- The Fabric -

Your **Thoughts** shape your beliefs.
Your **Beliefs** become your intentions.
Your **Intentions** create your actions.
Your **Actions** reinforce your **thoughts.**

Now that we have picked up a hint about what is affecting our thoughts, let us look further at how our thoughts affect our beliefs, creating both our intentions and our actions. Every time you do something, you obviously affect the world around you. No scientific studies are really needed to see this. You can witness the effects of your actions on the world around you with your own eyes.

In the field of mathematics as well as other disciplines of science exists the widely accepted "chaos theory," from which a concept known as the "butterfly effect" states that a 'small change at one place in a nonlinear system can result in large differences to a later state.' [1]

Models of the "butterfly effect" indicate that every decision we make and everything we do affects and changes the world around us – as every tiny decision we make will create a different outcome, which in turn begets another decision that creates another outcome with its own chain of events to follow. Scripture explains:

"Whoever turns a sinner from the error of his way will save him from death and cover a multitude of sins." James 5:20

This effect was verified by a famous quantum particle physics experiment. In a demonstration in which electrons were passed through a double-slit apparatus, it was determined that there are various probable locations for where an individual electron will strike a detection screen behind the apparatus. But once one has hit, there is no longer any probability that it will strike somewhere else.

As we gathered earlier from quantum theories, each and every particle also exists as a wave of energy. Those who subscribe to this theory – known as the "Copenhagen Interpretation" – claim "that a wave function also involves the various probabilities that a given event will proceed to certain different outcomes." [2] But when one or another of those outcomes manifests, the other probabilities no longer exist. So whether we are talking about the particle state or the wave state of all particles, the "butterfly effect" still applies.

When we couple Freud's theory that states all of our actions are directed by our subconscious intentions with the Copenhagen Interpretation that states every decision or action we make creates an outcome that rules out the possibility of all other outcomes (that potentially existed prior to our decision or action manifesting itself), then we can see that it is from within each of us that a subconscious motivation (that we are not consciously aware of) is affecting and shaping the world around us. In other words, we are physically changing the world around us by our decisions and actions, which we aren't even aware of why we made them in the first place.

Seriously! So again we ask: What existed within us that led us to make the decisions we have made? Who or what is actually guiding us and shaping our physical world?

Up until recently, what occurs within our bodies that creates our subconscious intentions has not been easily recognized. But, with technological advances in science, we can gain a clearer understanding of how we are guided from within.

To begin with, we can now see that as we move and act in the physical world, the chemical reactions taking place within our cells and between our cells are immeasurable – they are endless. Further, we can see that the chemically-laden hormones released in our brains as we move and interact influence and control us in ways we were not consciously aware of before.

We have also now become aware of the fact that whatever results from our actions will also affect us internally, changing our body chemistry again.

"Blessed ... are those who hear the word of God and obey it."
Luke 11:28

Let's look at one example. If you were to hit someone, chemicals such as adrenaline and cortisol would be released and would cover the cells throughout your body. If the person you hit responds by hitting you back, more chemicals would be generated that are associated with feelings of anger and pain. Or, if they cower, or ask for your mercy, a different set of chemicals would get dumped into your bloodstream.

And as we learned about the release of chemicals by our thoughts, if the same actions and reactions are repeated enough, our cells will build openings specifically for those "drugs." Then, without even being consciously aware of it, our bodies will be intentionally setting up situations where those chemicals can be released again to feed the cravings of our cells. 3

In a sense, our every decision leading to our every behavior is due to some sort of chemical addiction of our cells!

Yes, it turns out we are less in control of our own thoughts than we realize... Our thoughts (which in turn create our actions) are shaped by our chemical cravings. Moreover, because of the "Butterfly Effect," it turns out that our chemical addictions have shaped the world.

Think about it: If underlying every decision is our subconscious intention that is created by our chemical craving, and, in turn, our every decision affects the world around us, after having selected from infinite possibilities, then we have materialized what we have become addicted to – what we have fed our cells.

This is why Jesus said to his disciple, **"If you love me, feed my lambs." John 21:15**

What are your cells being fed? Whatever it is, as we learned earlier, your every cell will lead you to do whatever it takes to produce more of it. Once they become fed by it, they will crave more of it. And subconsciously you will somehow set up a situation for yourself that will ultimately provide you with the release of more of the same. You are being led by "spirits" – or chemical energies – of all kinds that your cells are feeding on, that you are not even aware are guiding you.

"Therefore, rid yourselves of all malice and all deceit, hypocrisy, envy, and slander of every kind. Like new-born babies, crave pure spiritual milk."
1 Peter 2:1

"There's an invisible world. It's a world of power. It's a world of possibility... It's a world of spirit. It controls everything." Pat Robertson, *A Life of Miracles*

"Every one who is seriously involved in the pursuit of science becomes convinced that a spirit is manifest in the laws of the Universe..." Albert Einstein

Spirit: non-quantifiable substance or <u>energy</u> present individually in all living things. -From *Wikipedia.com* 4

Spirit: the fundamental, emotional, and activating principle of a person; will. -From *Dictionary.com* 5

I hope we can agree to the notion that, for lack of a more scientific term at the time the Bible was written, the chemical energies we are now realizing to be what moves us from within were once referred to as "spirits"; and that today we can use the terms "spirit" and "energy" interchangeably as we continue with this discussion. Some "spirits" I may even refer to as "toxins," which just sounds a little more scientific than "evil spirits." But in essence, if they are not from God, they are the same. Along those lines, when the Bible speaks of the spirit with a capitol S, it is referring to the Holy Spirit of God.

"Those who live according to the sinful nature have their minds set on what that nature desires; but those who live in accordance with the Spirit have their minds set on what the Spirit desires. The mind of the sinful man is death, but the mind controlled by the Spirit is life."
Romans 8:5

Do you ever see people making the same mistakes over and over? After realizing this cycle we are all in, we can see that they have been led over and over by the same spirit – they have become chemically addicted to the energy resulting from their situations.

But now we can see that changing our actions involves more than we knew. To break the cycle we are in actually requires a chemical withdrawal.

Withdrawing from whatever chemical you have been feeding your cells can be very painful. Just as starvation would feel to our bodies, the many cells that have been feeding on these chemicals will feel like they are starving.

This emptiness from the lack of energy they had grown to absorb so readily, no longer being supplied to them, will cause them pain. And pain is something most of us intentionally try to avoid. It is human nature to seek pleasure and to avoid pain.

Breaking old habits involves a painful withdrawal before we can free ourselves – it is not easy. In many cases it is the most difficult thing we could ever go through.

But, when those habits are negative, not of God, and are keeping you stuck in a cycle that breeds sickness and death, it is worth it to break them! And there is a way. On the other side of the withdrawal period is the life that God has truly planned for us.

One of the most difficult things for me to surrender to God was a relationship that I had been investing in for years. At the time I was led to fully surrender to God's will and to fully trust Him, I had the hardest time giving this one thing up. I had placed all my hopes in it, and had relied on it for so much. But I knew God was calling me to surrender it to Him. I knew I needed to relinquish what I felt was my control of it. What a battle this was for me. But finally with tears, I submitted. I handed this relationship up to God for His will to be done in it. Instantly, I felt Him say to me, although not in any exact words, just something in the same essence of "Good job. Now you can have it back." And He handed it right back to me, only without the stronghold it once had over me.

I felt like I had experienced a moment similar to Abraham, being asked to give up his son. God tested his heart in a sense, and when he had surrendered, God gave him amazing grace, and showed him a better way. As if to prepare us for the ultimate choice we will need to make, He allows us to submit and then find out that it was all okay. But the first submission requires strong faith. From there forward, once we have discovered the trustworthiness of God, surrendering over and over is not a problem, but rather a valuable ability. On the other side of our surrender, God provides something even better.

"Forget the former things; do not dwell on the past. See I am doing a new thing. Do you not perceive it?"
Isaiah 43:18

"From now on I will tell you of new things, of hidden things unknown to you."
Isaiah 48:6

"Many are the plans in a man's heart, but it is the Lords purpose that prevails."
Proverbs 19:21

"He who trusts in the lord will prosper."
Proverbs 28:25

There lies ahead a time of distress unparalleled by anything we have ever known on our planet. In preparation, God allows his children to suffer some, in order to learn who they can ultimately put their trust in. Is it in the world, in someone here? Who is the one that can truly save them in the end? Without an opportunity to learn this, and to really see it confirmed in tough times, we could miss out when it really counts. So be glad if you've been tested and found strength in God. Rejoice in your suffering that you have been counted worthy to receive this lesson from God in order to prepare you for later. He loves you.

"There is no fear in love. But perfect love drives out fear."
1 John 4:18

You need not worry about failing, being unloved, being rejected, or being unwanted. The truth is you are perfectly loved, fully accepted, and so preciously sought after by your heavenly Father that nothing else matters. And God's promises never fail.

"My grace is sufficient for you, for my power is made perfect in weakness."
2 Corinthians 12:9

"But this happened that we might not rely on ourselves but on God." 2 Corinthians 1:9

"Therefore since Christ suffered in his body, arm yourselves also with the same attitude, because he who has suffered in his body is done with sin."
1 Peter 4:1

"Therefore we do not lose heart. Though outwardly we are wasting away, yet inwardly we are being renewed day by day. For our light and momentary troubles are achieving for us an eternal glory that far outweighs them all."
2 Corinthians 4:16

"I consider that our present sufferings are not worth comparing to the glory that will be revealed in us."
Romans 8:18

"For the creation was subjected to frustration, not by its own choice, but by the will of the one who subjected it, in hope that the creation itself will be

liberated from its bondage to decay and brought into the glorious freedom of the children of God." Romans 8:20

As humans we can become addicted to anything and everything. Sadly, one of the most pervasive problems we suffer from in our world today stems from the addiction to the chemicals associated with sex outside of God's design.

Oxytocin, which we mentioned earlier, and dopamine are feel-good chemicals released in the body (created as a result of our physical interactions and by our thoughts), and are highly addictive. This addiction could be subconsciously responsible for almost every decision the unaware addict makes.

When a man ejaculates, his brain signals the release of huge quantities of oxytocin into the bloodstream. 6 That is quite a chemical rush. Similar chemical scenarios take place for women during and after sex.

It may be the most powerful way to keep two people together, as they literally become chemically addicted to each other and to the results of their interactions. Certainly this is why God created this process to occur exclusively between a husband and a wife who are committed to each other for the duration of their earthly lives.

But, if sex occurs outside of God's design, and the partners separate, the resulting split is often a painful time like none other.

Once a cycle is begun that leads to the release of these chemicals, it will become the subconscious effort of all of the cells needing to feed on them again to lead that individual to repeat the same action.

The obvious lesson in this would be *not* to start a cycle outside of marriage. This act is more than just a slippery slope; it is a huge valley of glue! Climbing out of it will not be easy.

"You have heard it said, 'Do not commit adultery.' But I tell you that anyone who looks at a woman with lust fully has already committed adultery with her in his heart."
Matthew 5:27

As Jesus points out in this passage, the thought of the act alone is even enough to create the sin and its consequences.

Even chemicals created by our thoughts alone, if outside of marriage, need to be avoided to prevent an improper and painful addiction from developing. When released as a result of these thoughts, these chemicals will be paired in our minds with them, leading us to crave more of the thoughts that create this release.

But, in the *right* context, one could call them the chemicals of procreation. They keep us powerfully connected, and keep us alive as they help to ensure the continuation of our species. Unfortunately, they also appear to be some of the most powerful weapons that the enemy of our lives has when he uses them for his purposes – to keep us from the life that God has planned for us.

As we will see later, the devil cannot create anything, but can only twist or confuse the creation of God to lead us down the path that ultimately ends in death.

With the ability to see these chemical energies and their effects, he knows how powerful they are, and uses them in perverted, unnatural, and twisted ways to accomplish his goal of our destruction. He uses our subconscious need for these chemicals to sell us on his lies.

Apart from our foods (or drugs which have been deemed illegal), no other chemicals seem to be as highly addictive. Almost every path we find ourselves on can be traced back to the pursuit of sex and the chemicals our bodies are craving. However, this "pursuit" is occurring on a subconscious level, so it's not as obvious as it sounds.

To see how Satan uses sex to accomplish his goals, we have to first understand Pavlov's findings about his famous dogs. In a widely known experiment on behavior, Ivan Pavlov, a Russian physiologist, conditioned his dogs to salivate at the ring of a bell.

How could he create this physiological response – salivating – with the sound of a bell when the response is not normal for the natural design of the dogs? He accomplished this by systematically pairing the sound of a ringing bell with the delivery of their food.

The delivery of their food should, and does, elicit the natural response of salivating in order to prepare their mouths and digestive systems for the impending meal.

In Pavlov's experiment, after many times of connecting the sound of the bell with the delivery of the food, the dogs' brains built connections between the two events. After enough pairings, the food didn't even need to be present for the dogs to begin to salivate when they heard the bell ring.

We as humans are not much different from Pavlov's dogs in this sense. Our brains are making connections and associations between things we hear, see, smell, and touch every minute of every day.

It is part of our design so that we can learn to navigate safely in the world, and also to provide us with health and life, as God intends.

Our bodies will, of course, continue to crave the release of the chemicals involved in sex including oxytocin and dopamine, so we become led (subconsciously) to fulfill the chemical cravings that we desire. And whatever our minds have paired with the release of these chemicals will become what we seek.

In other words, whatever our minds have associated with sex, we will be searching for subconsciously.

Further, whatever we may have paired with the object or objects that we associate with sex become luring, and then what ever we may have associated with those objects become alluring.

The subconscious pairings we make can become so far removed from the actual target that we end up making decisions about things for which we have absolutely no conscious reason. We are led to do one thing that we have been conditioned to associate with another thing that we have associated with something else, that we at some point learned leads to the release of oxytocin and dopamine.

As powerful as this is, it is understandable that much of what we do and the choices we make as humans can be traced back to our desire to feed the craving of our cells for these chemicals.

Knowing its power over us, Satan uses sex all the time to lead us astray. He pairs sex and the chemical release it will bring with just about anything. "Sex sells." Material goods are almost always portrayed in advertising alongside music, sights, and sounds that our brains will associate with sex. It is the advertisers' hope that if we view these pairings enough we will be led to purchase their items in our never-ending subconscious effort to feed our cells, so to speak.

"For Satan himself masquerades as an angel of light. It is not surprising, then, if his servants masquerade as servants of righteousness. Their end will be what their actions deserve."
2 Corinthians 11:14

What is even worse is when the devil pairs unnatural objects or situations with sexual arousal. No experiment needs to be conducted for us to realize that if you were to pair an object or a situation with sexual stimulation over and over, a person will begin to associate that object or environment with sex. Before you know it, the unnatural object or situation will create the physiological response elicited by sexual arousal simply because it had been paired with the act of sex often enough (the same way that Pavlov's dogs salivated to the sound of a bell just because a bell was paired with their food over and over). This is how Satan and those under his influence entice people to develop fetishes with unnatural situations or objects.

It is one of the enemy's many ways of twisting God's design that leads people into a life of sin, shame, suffering, despair and eventually death. It is being used in ways to make associations that create horrific cycles of sin, even in children. It is an invisible (yet very real) trap we can fall into as our human bodies crave the chemicals that God intended for us to use to enjoy healthy lives, and to provide for the assurance of future generations. But instead we see the world being corrupted by the twisting of our chemical needs by those who want to use and abuse us and/or sell us something. And we buy into the lies we are told that lead us down destructive paths.

Why have we handed the authority of sex over to Satan? This incredible gift along with the chemicals it releases is God's gift. It is His creation, and when we hand the authority of this act back to Him, it will be blessed beyond our imagination.

The truth is we are whole and loved beyond our physical need of any worldly chemicals. God can, and will, supply all of our needs. We will soon understand how. But for now, as we have clearly seen, the loving instructions of God in the Bible are for our own good. We can take note that God's word says:

"Flee from sexual immorality. All other sins a man commits are outside his body, but he who sins sexually sins against his own body."
1 Corinthians 6:18

"Do you not know that the wicked will not inherit the kingdom of God? Do not be deceived: Neither the sexually immoral nor idolaters not adulterers nor male prostitutes nor homosexual offenders nor thieves nor the greedy nor drunkards nor slanderers nor swindlers will inherit the kingdom of God. And that is what some of you were. But you were washed, you were sanctified, you were justified in the name of the Lord Jesus Christ and by the Spirit of our God."
1 Corinthians 6:12

On that note, I want to be careful to mention that we should not judge others. This book is about *your* personal health and *your* personal spiritual life. Jesus tells us that we will be judged by God with the same measure that we judge others.

"There is no one righteous, not even one..."

Romans 3:10

But we *do* need to judge what is leading us. In John 8:44, Jesus "warns of the reality of Satan's murderous and deceitful influence." (NIV Study Bible)

"If anyone causes one of these little ones who believes in me to sin, it would be better for him to be thrown into the sea with a large millstone tied around his neck." Mark 9:42

The reality is not just with sex but with whatever you are doing habitually, you are, without even knowing it, creating ties and addictions to those actions. The chemicals released in the performing of an action and in the resulting effects of that action become what your cells are feeding on and what you are "covered" with. They form an invisible cyclical bond with your physical body.

Our repeated actions and reactions can literally establish a stronghold over us. We become held and addicted to our situations in an invisible, though very real, way; as if in bondage as a slave to whatever has mastered us. We are all prisoners of this law and of the sin it reveals.

If we want to change, it becomes very difficult. To free ourselves from our actions, we have to free ourselves of the situations to which we have become enslaved. To change our actions, and our outcomes, we have to rid ourselves chemically of all those toxins produced by our interactions and thoughts.

In addition, it is not enough to just get rid of the chemicals. We have to *replace* them with something good. If not, another toxin will just take its place.

For example, a person may rid himself of a sex addiction and the power it had over his life; but then as the pain of the withdrawal begins, he may choose to fill the empty spaces with alcohol or drugs.

"When an evil spirit comes out of a man, it goes through arid places seeking rest and does not find it. Then it says 'I will return to the house I left.' When it arrives, it finds the house swept clean and put in order. Then it goes and takes seven other spirits more wicked than itself and they go in and live there. And the final condition of that man is worse than the first."
Luke 11:24

In similar fashions, people may free themselves from bad relationships and find the resulting empty spaces so painful that they will choose yet another bad relationship to ease the acute pain, setting themselves up for an even worse outcome.

So the question becomes: What exists that is good and always available to replace the chemical energy of the situations we need to break free from? (We will soon see.)

"Do not let sin reign in your mortal body so that you obey its evil desires. Do not offer the parts of your body to sin, as instruments of wickedness, but rather, offer yourselves to God, as those who have been brought from death to life; and offer the parts of your body to righteousness. For sin shall not be your master, because you are not under law, but under grace."
Romans 6:14

One universal law at work in this world is that for every action there is a reaction. For every good act, there comes some type of reward. And for every action that is bad, there comes a punishment. Everything creates a consequence for itself. It is part of the fabric of this universe that God created. It is derived from the laws of physics. Some also call it karma, or the law of cause and effect. It goes hand in hand with the cyclical nature in which God set the entire universe in motion.

From the moment of conception we are in constant back-and-forth communication with our environment. We, even as embryos, send out an electric impulse, and one is received back. We listen and respond with growth to signals from our own DNA. One of my brilliant psychology professors once explained to us (as I recall) that you really cannot separate nature from nurture. Even as we begin as a single cell – sending out signals to our environment and receiving them back – our genes *are* our first environment; as our cells replicate and reproduce, they communicate with each other to direct our growth in the womb. Our "nature and nurture" are intertwined as we become a part of a constant interaction with the world around us that is never without a reciprocal effect. 7 For every action, there appears to be an equally proportioned reaction, which in turn creates another reaction, and the cycle never ends.

We can visibly witness these cycles everywhere: the water cycle of evaporation; condensation and precipitation; the circadian rhythms of sleep and wake cycles; the cycle of oxygen breathing animals producing carbon dioxide for plants who in turn release oxygen for the consumption of animals; and etcetera.

There's the nitrogen cycle, the carbon cycle, and within families and across generations we see cycles of abuse, where abused children later become abusers of their own children. There is a cycle of pain and suffering and, some believe, a cycle of birth and death.

Everything is tangled into interlocking rings of cycle after cycle (from the microscopic to the macroscopic in size) that build upon themselves, weaving together into this intricate, thick fabric of our non-static universe.

Throughout history people and societies have searched for ways to attempt to peacefully keep themselves in these cycles. As if trying to understand and play the most intricate game of chess ever created, we attempt to maneuver ourselves through life. We try to do good, hoping for a good outcome, and often even strive for perfection. We weave through these cycles trying to keep ourselves successful in them, as if the goal of our lives were located somewhere within this fabric we are trapped in.

But we are living in a fallen world. No one can be perfect and receive a perfect result all the time. The current fallen nature of our world sets us all up for failure from the very beginning. We inherit negative cycles derived from our parents' and grandparents' actions and choices, and from the chemicals we fed on in the womb.

As a part of God's universal creation, we are all in these cycles together, and we all suffer the consequences of our wrong actions, and the wrong actions of generations before us.

But, also as a part of God's creation, and His great plan, there is One who breaks the very fabric of these laws. There is one who lived in perfect, holy interaction with the world around Him. There is one who sacrificed His holy life, and took for us the pain and consequences of *our* sins, so that we would never again have to suffer from the results they would have manifested in our lives. So we never again have to feel guilt or shame. So that we can be completely free to live and to love. Jesus' sacrifice on the cross was more powerful than the fabric of the world.

At the time of Jesus' death, the Bible says, the curtain was torn:

"At that moment the curtain of the temple was torn in two from top to bottom. The earth shook and the rocks split." Matthew 27:51

He tore the interlocking cyclical fabric of the universe! His unswerving, unfaltering dedication to this plan of God for us opened the way. Despite the suffering it required, His overcoming of the world and its lures, His unbelievably selfless sacrifice of His life, this act that is beyond all worldly comprehension, created a tear and a riff in space and time, halting the consequences that would have been reciprocated in their cyclical tracks!

Like a lightning bolt that separates the air on either side of it, He created a path that diverts the energy flow of the ways of the world on either side of it. He broke the cycles. He opened a pathway instead, which like a river of new energy flows, connecting this world to the everlasting source of God.

And, as if that weren't enough, by His resurrection Jesus overcame the last of the strongholds. He overcame death itself. He literally showed us that there is life after death, a spiritual life that Jesus' resurrected body allowed us to see with our own eyes.

"Stop doubting and believe... because you have seen me, you have believed; blessed are those who have not seen and yet have believed."
John 20:27

There does exist an energy stronger and more powerful than any of the chemical energies in this world that may have taken a fleeting stronghold over your life. And the temporary hold over us by every enemy to God will be broken in the end. God is triumphant. It has already been spoken. And, as we will see, His word is irrevocable.

No matter how big or small, we all have something or someone that has us hooked, holding us back from the life that God has planned for us. My guess is you don't even have to look that deep; you already know this. It has caused you to stumble and sin in your life.

But, the truth is, you are forgiven. By the sacrifice of Jesus, your past is wiped clean. So be encouraged. There is something far better waiting to fill you, and to lead you in the direction of life.

We see earlier in scripture that Jesus was the master of breaking all cycles, even as He walked in human form. He taught us to **"Love your enemies, do good to those who hate you, bless those who curse you, pray for those who mistreat you, If someone strikes you on one cheek, turn to him the other also..." Luke 6:27**

He is the cycle breaker. To free ourselves of our strongholds and turn to the blessed, perfect life God has planned for us, we just need to let Him in. We have to stop submitting ourselves to the world, and truly believe God instead, giving our authority back to Him and allowing His power to work within us. It is by *His* power *within* us that we have the ability to overcome anything. We will talk more about the science behind this in a later chapter; for now just know that God has designed you and has a perfect plan for your life, and *He* will give you the power to overcome any hurdle or obstacle the devil puts in your way to attempt to thwart you from living it.

"For it is God who works in you to will and act according to his good purpose."
Philippians 2:13

"You, dear children, are from God and have overcome them, because the one who is in you is greater than the one who is in the world."
1 John 4:4

"For I know the plans I have for you, declares the Lord, plans to prosper you and not to harm you, plans to give you hope and a future. Then you will call upon me and come and pray to me, and I will listen to you. You will seek me and find me when you seek me with all you heart. I will be found by you, declares the Lord, and will bring you back from captivity."
Jeremiah 29:11

5

- Baptism -

"To this end I labor, struggling with all his energy, which so powerfully works in me."
Colossians 1: 29

In the same way that God first gave us the seed of life in the womb for our physical bodies, He is also the giver of the seed of life for our spiritual beings. He gives us His Holy Spirit. It descends upon us the Bible explains. From that point forward our flesh is freed from and cleansed from all our past addictions and we become covered in Christ, able to move with His power leading the way.

Note what Jesus said at one point to His disciples:

"I am going to send you what my Father has promised; but stay in the city until you have been clothed with power from on high." Luke 24:49

Through Christ's sacrifice of his physical body, we were promised His Spirit. And His Spirit in us is also a promise, a guarantee, that by Him working in us, we will be led home. He is the one who carved the path to heaven.

Take note that the first connection is made from there to us. We will see later that in a quantum mechanical demonstration, that it is always in that order. God is truly in control.

In the example of baptism, it is the Holy Spirit that descends upon us. At that point, we now have our path carved. We then know the way home. This is a remarkable turning point. It is only *symbolized* by the act of baptism in water. The actual baptism of the Holy Spirit can happen anywhere at any time.

"I baptize you with water for repentance. But after me will come one who is more powerful than I, whose sandals I am not fit to carry. He will baptize you with the Holy Spirit..." from John the Baptist in Matthew 3:11

6

- Stay Connected -

"For I am convinced that neither death nor life, neither angels nor demons, neither the present nor the future, nor any powers, neither height nor depth, nor anything else in all creation, will be able to separate us from the love of God that is in Christ Jesus our Lord." Romans 8:38

We are connected through Christ – connected to the realm of God where all things are possible and where there is truly life.

In the next chapter we will learn about the power of our focus on an idea or thought. Even without the science behind it, common sense seems to tell us that if we stay focused on how to live this life to its fullest, and in a sense how to use God's thoughts or principles to make money here, or to live successfully here -or whatever the case may be, we have missed the point.

Although following God's authority *will* bless your life here and break the curse from Genesis that makes the Earth a place of labor and pain, we can't make that our aim. Thinking that a blessed life *here* is what is most important will only keep you focused on the here. We are blessed with the feeling of peace and rest when we observe the Sabbath here, and our fruits are awesome and wonderful as a result of believing and obeying God here. But, this happens only as a reminder or an example to demonstrate the real glorious place of rest and the amazing feast that is to come for us who believe.

Instead of staying focused on how wonderful the outcome of obeying God is here, we need to shift our mindset to know that our real treasures await us in heaven.

"But godliness with contentment is great gain. For we brought nothing into the world, and we can take nothing out of it. But if we have food and clothing, we will be content with that. People who want to get rich fall into temptation and a trap and into many foolish and harmful desires that plunge men into ruin and destruction. For the love of money is a root of all kinds of evil."
1 Timothy 6:6

Other questions to consider as we break free of the cycles of the world are: How do we really connect to God's energy and stay connected? And how do we ensure the strength of our connection to Him and trust that it will remain stronger than any of our ties here?

The first step is to become baptized with the Holy Spirit. Then, what God has shown me is a picture of channels connecting our souls to his realm, like the vines of a plant connecting every branch to its root, or the veins in the body connecting every cell to the heart. We strengthen our pathway to the Creator every time we connect to him in prayer through the name of Jesus.

Each time you think about God (*really* think about Him), picture in your mind that you are creating an invisible connection to Him. To ensure you have begun to truly think of God, you should begin to feel a complete sense of awe and reverence mixed with humility and gratefulness (at least that is how I feel). How could we truly be thinking of the Almighty Creator of the universe, powerful yet full of grace and love and compassion for us lost sheep, without feeling this way. Once you know who you are praying to, once you are focused on Him, then in His name you can begin to pray.

When Jesus taught us to pray, He said to begin with: **"Our Father in heaven, hallowed be your name..." (Matthew 6:9)** It's all about Him. Beginning with a connection to Him – by thinking on Him and His name – is the key. Once you are really thinking of Him and you pray in the name of Jesus Christ, and in the peace of the Holy Spirit, you create a connection between you and the spiritual dimension of heaven.

Like an upside-down vine, God's energy in heaven is the source or root of the plant. And every time someone connects his mind to God, an invisible branch appears that connects him to the source. The more times we connect, just like a path in the woods that becomes easier to follow the more times it is traveled, the clearer our path and the stronger our connection to His realm become.

In my attempt to describe to a friend how prayers actually work, I told him to imagine that when he speaks words through the tiny holes in his cell phone, those words travel through the roof of his home, pass through the atmosphere, and are received by a satellite in outer space. Then his words are redirected back down through the sky to land in the ear of the exact person he intended for them to reach.

It's incredible but true. We can't see this happening, but by its results we can conclude it works. In the same way, when we pray to God in heaven, our words travel to their intended destination, creating that connection through space and time from our four-dimensional world to heaven.

As we quietly listen for a reply, we allow another connection to develop. The more often we repeat this, the stronger those connections become, until those connections develop into well-traveled pathways where energy flows effortlessly back and forth between us and God, through the "gate" and through the "vine" that are the energy of Jesus Christ.

Just like the little children in the twin study, who were open to giving and receiving the energy flow which resulted in their ability to share their thoughts, we open ourselves to God's energy flow when we are free of shame and guilt and other toxins that keep us closed off; which, by his death and through our baptism, Jesus gave us the power to rid ourselves of.

Once we accept His sacrifice for us and truly believe we are freed from sins, we are unveiled and opened, in the light. We can openly and unashamedly pray to our awesome God, connecting and strengthening our pathway to heaven.

This next study demonstrates these pathways on a microscopic level with this same concept occurring in plants.

In the spring of 2007, a team of scientists led by Graham Fleming, deputy director of the Lawrence Berkeley National Laboratory, reported a revolutionary quantum science phenomenon when they were able to observe photosynthesis in plants using ultrafast lasers. They discovered that the interaction between the sun's energy and the chlorophyll molecules in a bacterium exemplifies these pathways we just spoke about. In addition, this study brings awareness to what quantum scientists call the "superposition phenomenon." [1]

First, let's take a look at the "superposition phenomenon." These scientists discovered that the exact same particle of light energy, the photon, existed in more than one place – seemingly available in a state of multiple potentials – before it materialized where it was ultimately determined to be. For the first time scientists were actually able to observe – with the aid of their high tech equipment – this difficult to imagine phenomenon. In the state right before it is set in its materialized place, the same little photon can be seen existing all about in what is called its "superposition." Then, once the particle materializes, it comes together in its "collapsed" state, in the place where we ultimately observe it and where it can be seen in our material realm.

So, consider if you will, in the same way that scientists observed the energy of the photon existing in several different states or infinite possibilities at once, so too does the energy of God. We call this *omnipresence*. God exists as the Father, the Son and the Holy Spirit. He is the creator, the judge, the restorer, and the redeemer. God is love. God is light – in many available states at once. He exists in a "superposition."

"With man this is impossible, but with God, all things are possible." Matthew 19:26

According to Skip Moen's book, *Words to Lead By*, when used as in the scripture quoted above, the Greek word for *with* is *para*, which is defined as: *in the proximity of*. But by using the word *with*, some of the original Greek writer's meaning is lost.

Moen explains that this scripture really means that as we stand in the proximity of men, we see things from man's perspective. 2

In light of this quantum principle, that would mean we see things already in their collapsed, materialized state. Jesus explains that when we are "with" God, however, or "standing in the proximity of God," seeing things from where He resides, we see all things as potential energy, existing in their superposition, where there are infinite possibilities, where *all* things are possible.

"With man this is impossible, but with God, all things are possible." Matthew 19:26

In the study, like a wave of potentiality, the light energy existed in multiple states before it took on its selected material position. And almost instantly it appeared where it was intended to go.

According to the researchers, from this superposition, existing everywhere, the photon's energy was, in a sense, able to test all of the possible reaction pathways within the various chlorophyll molecules. "The most efficient pathway was then selected, and energy was transferred through the bacterium as the superposition collapsed."

The scientists concluded that the energy existed in multiple states, and then chose the pathway that was most accessible and efficient for it to travel to the destined molecule for its consumption. 3

In the same way God exists in these many states at once, scientists were able to photograph the energy waves of the photon (the tiniest bit of a light particle that still retains all of the properties of light) existing in many, possibly infinite places at once. And, in the same way that the photon tested pathways and chose the most efficient path before materializing within the chlorophyll molecules, we can then imagine the invisible pathways we create every time we connect with God in prayer.

One could also compare the energy of the light in this study to the energy of God – as light is of the same essence as God; with both being the source of the energy that sustains life as we know it.

"God is light." 1 John 1:5

**"When Jesus spoke again to the people he said, "I am the light of the world. Whoever follows me will never walk in darkness, but will have the light of life."
John 8:12**

**"For with you is the fountain of life; in your light we see light."
Psalm 36:9**

We will talk more about the superposition phenomenon and discuss the photon's relation to God in more detail later.

But for now, please note that *our* brains are designed similarly in structure as the plant in that observation. Brain cells communicate with each other by sending and receiving electrically charged chemical ions. The tiny contact point where the exchange takes place between brain cells is called the synapse. When we learn something new, we create branches by forming new synaptic connections between cells. Just like the reaction pathways within the chlorophyll molecules in the plants, neuron pathways, shaped like trees in our brains, grow new branches as we live and learn. Some branches grow stronger with repeated use.

"As our developing brain blooms and prunes connections, it has to decide which ones to fix permanently in place, and which to ones to dissolve. Preserving what's useful and killing the rest. How does it determine what's useful? Whatever we use most." 4

Just like photons select the most efficient pathways throughout the various plant molecules, the most efficient pathways for the transfer of energy through our brain cells are carved out, pruned, and strengthened as we choose what thoughts and actions to repeat.

And we strengthen our connection to God's realm through our open belief in Christ. It is Jesus who is the vine that connects us to God through the great chasm that exists between our world and heaven. God's energy decides where it will go. It is God who does the work in us and around us.

All we have to do is believe in order to be open to it. We will see in a later chapter how our unbelief and the resulting sin prevent us from seeing the result of God's intention: His perfect design.

But, by our belief we can open those pathways to Him and strengthen those connections above all others.

"I am the true vine, and my Father is the gardener. He cuts off every branch in me that bears no fruit, while every branch that does bear fruit he prunes so that it will be even more fruitful."
John 15:1

"If the part of the dough offered as first-fruits is holy, then the whole batch is holy; if the root is holy, so are the branches."
Romans 11:16

Throughout the small history of time that we as Homo sapiens, (Latin for 'knowing man') have possessed a spiritual soul within our bodies, from the time of Adam and Eve through today, an outline of those who believed and were open to trusting God can be read about in the Bible. It began with Abraham who was the first to have and to demonstrate complete faith in the one true living God, although he could not see Him. Then God spoke a promise through the prophet Samuel. God promised that a descendent of David's would have all power and authority and would build an everlasting kingdom with all of His offspring, referring to both physical offspring that believed in Him and those who would be included by their belief alone. That descendent, as was disclosed to Mary by an angel generations later, was Jesus.

It is now, by believing in Him, we are able to make those connections and to ultimately become a part of God's kingdom of heaven. This has been the design of God for our redemption since the beginning. It's all about faith.

"If some of the branches have been broken off, and you, through a wild olive shoot, have been grafted in among the others and now share in the nourishing sap from the olive root, do not boast over those branches. If you do, consider this: You do not support the root, but the root supports you. You will say then 'Branches were broken off so that I could be grafted in.' Granted. But

they were broken off because of unbelief, and you, stand by faith. Do not be arrogant, but be afraid. For if God did not spare the natural branches, he will not spare you, either. Consider therefore the kindness and sternness of God: sternness to those who fell. But kindness to you, provided that you continue in his kindness. Otherwise, you also will be cut off. And if they do not persist in unbelief, they will be grafted in, for God is able to graft them in again. After all, if you were cut out of an olive tree that is wild by nature and contrary to nature were grafted into a cultivated olive tree, how much more readily will these, the natural branches, be grafted in to their own olive tree."
Romans 11:17

Get grafted in, and stay connected by staying clothed in Christ's humility, grace, forgiveness and love.

But above all, just believe.

7

- Words -

When I was at one of the worst points in my recovery, I was fatigued and exhausted, lying in bed with heart failure that had yet to be diagnosed. At the time, I thought I must have been just recovering from the stroke still, and therefore hadn't been to see a cardiologist yet. In any case, I was having great difficulty with just breathing. Fluid had likely built up in my lungs as a result of the inefficiency of my heart in pumping the blood through my body. Every breath seemed to require more energy than my lungs actually had. Each breath was an effort and one that seemed my lungs were growing more and more weary of making. One night, this became especially bad. My children were already sleeping, and calling for an ambulance was dismissed in my thoughts at that time, as I didn't want the trauma of it to scare them or to create a problem for anyone else. Everyone I knew had their own battles to deal with, and I didn't want my burdens to add to anyone else's. Looking back, I probably should have sought medical help, but my reasoning was also very weak at that time as well. So I just prayed as I drifted to sleep. I prayed that God would give my body the strength to continue breathing through the night, and that He would keep me and my children safe.

The Lord blessed me with an experience that night that I will never forget. I will do my best to share it, for what it is worth to you, but words hardly can explain it. It was an event that was without dialogue. So to describe it, I have to search for the words that best fit the account of what happened. Anyway, that night, as my body lacked even the smallest amount of energy necessary to carry on its most basic of functions (supplying oxygen to its cells so they can live), I was blessed with what people call an "out of body experience."

I felt, saw, and knew my soul was slowly leaving my body, and I felt myself drifting closer to the spiritual realm. The further away from the physical realm I got, the more peace I felt.

As I was first released from my body, in a panic I turned back to look at what I was leaving behind. Horrified to leave my children, my family and my responsibilities, I felt a sense of panic. But with each second that I slowly drifted closer to the Lord, waves of peace and comfort washed through me. The closer I got to the presence of our Almighty God, the more reassurance I felt. It was as if the closer I got, the more I *knew* that He had it all under control. As I drifted closer and closer into this encompassing peace, any doubts of His sovereignty over what I was leaving behind were washed away. I got to the place of total peace. I had no fear for the lives of my children that I had left in the world. I *knew* that He had them. Without words, I just knew beyond a shadow of a doubt that God Almighty had them right in the middle of His plan. I *knew* that there was nothing that I needed to do, because no matter what, they were already cared for and taken care of – that if it was God's plan for me to leave them, it would also be God's plan for someone still there to care for them. This thought was without any feeling of jealousy, regret, or any emotion. I simply knew at that point that God's plan was the ultimate best, best, best, and that nothing else mattered. I knew that nothing I could do would change it, nor would I ever in a million years want to. The place I was nearing was completely, wholly perfect. It was as if the closer I got to the surrounding and infiltrating presence of God that was so full of love, all my fears subsided. I was left with no fear, no worries, and no concerns – just peace, total restful, glorious, grateful peace.

Then, without words, it was as though I was given the option to return. Reasons for returning were 'shown' to me by means of both the sensation of visual images and of feelings that were combined into a pulse of understanding. The first "reason" I was asked to consider seemed like some sort of punishment I would receive if I didn't go back. I don't know exactly what it was, but I felt that something negative would happen to me if I didn't go back. Yet I also felt that in the wonderfully peace-filled place I was in, there was no punishment that could possibly exist that would be severe enough to motivate me to leave. The peace of God was too consuming. And the fear of punishment was dismissed as a motivation for returning. Then I was shown some kind of reward. I felt as though I would be highly esteemed and honored if I went back. This too was not motivation enough at all to prompt me to leave the glorious place I was in.

Then I was shown the little faces of my two children, and my heart overflowed with the spirit of love. It was only the energy of this love for them that was strong enough to motivate me to make the decision to come back. And instantly, I was back.

I share this story not because it is so outstanding or amazing. It is nothing compared to "near death" experiences that others have had and shared. But I share it because I later realized that it demonstrates the power of the driving force of love. And because it reminds me of John 3:16, **"For God so loved the world that he gave his one and only Son, that whoever believes in him shall not perish but have eternal life."**

For no other reason was God prompted to leave His place on high, and to come down to our hard cold planet, than because of His love for us, His children. Nothing else, no fear, no reward, nothing could have motivated me to leave the beautifully perfect realm I was in than the most powerful of all motivating forces: *love*.

Interestingly, I later read that psychology studies have repeatedly demonstrated that intrinsic motivation creates desired results better than extrinsic rewards in tasks that require higher level thinking (and that monetary rewards actually act as a distraction to completing the tasks.) [1]

As I recovered from the mini-stroke and was still suffering from heart failure, I was also given more affirmation of the strength of this internal driving force. It was all I could do at times to just breathe, I was so weak. Yet my bills had to be paid, and my children required clothes and food – I needed to work. So despite my failing health, I continued to perform work for my clients. My condition fluctuated enough that I could muster the energy necessary to get through meetings or whatever necessary for brief periods of time before needing to rest again and recover. Most days, I could only make it through the mornings, then I would lay in bed until school let out, use whatever energy I had left to care for the kids, cook dinner, do homework, etc., before crashing again. In any case, as much as I could prevent it, my clients were not aware of my health problems. I didn't want to lose them or their business over this. I had already cut back on the number of leads I could take – which were next to none – but I didn't want to give up the business I had already started. But sadly, every time my phone would ring, I would cringe. I just didn't have the strength to answer. My lungs barely had the energy to take breaths let alone hold an upbeat, positive conversation. So invariably my voicemail answered all my calls. I would listen to the message and then pray for the strength to return the call. During my prayer I would go over the reasons as to why I needed to return the call. Again, it was everything from fear of failure, and fear of poverty, to thoughts of reward and money and material things that went through my mind. But again, it was only the driving force of love that supplied enough energy to my cells to move me. I would literally have to view each individual client from God's viewpoint. In my prayers I would try to see them through His eyes, as God's children needing help in their endeavors. My heart would fill with love for them, and I would become motivated to help them only by this agape love that God would fill me with. It was the only place I could work from that provided me with enough energy. I couldn't muster the energy required to make calls from a place of fear, of hope for material things, of desire for money or anything else. Only when there was love within me to drive me was there physically enough force to move me to work.

"Dear friends, let us love one another, for love comes from God. Everyone who loves has been born of

God and knows God. Whoever does not love does not know God, because God is love."

1 John 4:7

So what does this have to do with words?

To explain this, let's start with what we have learned from the field of hypnotherapy. In a January 2001 article in *Psychology Today*, Harvard psychologist Deirdre Barrett wrote: "A hypnotic trance is not therapeutic in and of itself, but specific suggestions and images fed to clients in a trance can profoundly alter their behavior."

As noted earlier, we have subconscious awareness – knowing things that we aren't aware we know. And our bodies, controlled by biological forces and chemical interactions act, behave, and make decisions without our conscious minds even being aware. And we also know that thoughts or ideas in our minds affect our physical bodies.

Hypnotist William Carpenter's theory of the "ideo-motor" reflex explains this. He was able to observe that under certain circumstances, the mere idea of a muscle movement was sufficient to produce a reflexive contraction of the muscle involved. Hypnotist James Braid built on this finding and called it the "ideo-dynamic" response – meaning the power of an idea to create a response is not limited to muscular movement. For example, the idea of sucking a lemon actually induced the secretory response in his subjects. Braid went on to explain further that hypnotism operates by means of what he termed the "mono-ideo-dynamic" response. Long word, but basically it means that one single idea introduced with focused concentration during the hypnotic state will amplify the physical response that one idea would generate, while other ideas and thoughts are removed or dulled from the subject's awareness. With his studies, Braid was able to demonstrate that when a person is concentrating on a single idea or train of thought, called "monoideism," the effect of that particular idea is increased in the person's physical body. [2]

This explains why when I meditated on the words termed as the "fruits of the Spirit," the affects of the ideo-dynamic principle were visible in my physiological response, enhanced by my focus. This phenomenon is so powerful in fact that it has been used as an aid or alternative to chemical anesthesia during surgery. [3]

Some call this phenomenon "mind over matter." Others call it a psycho-somatic response. However we name it, God revealed this part of His design for us thousands of years ago to the apostles, which is why they have told us in scripture:

"Therefore... fix your thoughts on Jesus." Hebrews 3:1

"Let us fix our eyes on Jesus, the author and perfecter of our faith..." Hebrews 12:2

Clearly, when we are consciously focused on an idea our body physically responds. Why are we told to focus on Jesus? I will explain...

"And we also thank God continually because, when you received the word of God, which you heard from us, you accepted it not as the word of men, but as it actually is, the word of God, which is at work in you who believe."
1 Thessalonians 2:13

What we have learned from some of the greatest minds and writers of our time are ideas like: "Change your thoughts, and your outcome will be different"; "You will attract the outcome of your thoughts"; or, "Change your intentions, and you will change your destiny."

All of these statements are true. But if we don't start from the beginning, from the source, and change the **words**, whatever attempt we make to really change our thoughts, our intentions, or our actions will be temporary and futile. We have learned so much already, but that which is most important still lies ahead.

I've seen this demonstrated in several ways, but consider for a minute the order of development in this model:

Words make up your thoughts.
Your **Thoughts** shape your beliefs.
Your **Beliefs** become your intentions.
Your **Intentions** create your actions.
Your **Actions** become habits.
Your **Habits** become your character.

As we saw earlier, your habits will chemically reinforce your previously held thoughts, further creating the same actions and habits which ultimately become your character.

Your **Character** becomes who you are – **your identity**.

Your identity can be found in who you are in Christ, the one who overcame the world and has everlasting life with God. Or your identity can be found in earthly things which, as we know, will not last.

As we saw earlier, we have two paths: to put it simply, the paths that leads to death or to life. And the first step on either path is choosing which words we are going to allow to occupy our minds!

"I tell you the truth: Whoever hears my words and believes him who sent me has eternal life and will not be condemned; he has crossed over from death to life.
John 5:24

If we walk around in the world only hearing the words of the world, we stay trapped here, lost in the mess of our current fallen state. That's where I was until I finally heard the good news – I heard the words of God being spoken by a pastor whose church I thankfully stumbled upon. From there forward I began to connect to a state of redemption instead.

When we hear God's words and put them into action, those actions create a new cycle of energies that cleanse us and restore us, and eventually bring us, by the shepherding of our Lord Jesus, to a place where we completely overcome all of the sickness of the world. And in the end, we even overcome death, having crossed over into everlasting life as our Creator intended.

Again, as we know from scripture, each of our two natures, or two paths, is initially spawned by a seed. The first seed is the egg in your mother's womb that when fertilized grows into your earthy body. The second is the seed which God plants in you at the time of the baptism of the Holy Spirit. This seed grows into your spiritual body, which will continue to live even after your earthly body dies. The Bible also tells us that "the seed is the word of God." It draws the connection between the way a seed grows and the growing power of words.

One can either continue to mind seeds of the words produced by the world that are handed down to us as part of our earthly, sinful nature, and allow them to grow into thoughts, intentions, actions, and habits that lead us to suffering and destruction. Or we can choose to be baptized with the Holy Spirit and let the seed we receive at that point from God replace those words and forever alter the course of our lives as our thoughts, intentions, and actions lead us closer to God and to His Kingdom of everlasting life.

"For you have been born again, not of perishable seed, but of imperishable, through the living and enduring word of God.

For, 'All men are like grass, and all their glory is like the flowers of the field; the grass withers and the flowers fall. But the word of the Lord stands forever.'"

1 Peter 1:23

As we become broken by the world (like soil that has been tilled and loosened in preparation for a seed to be planted), we also become more prepared for the word of God to be planted deep inside of us.

Listen to this parable Jesus taught.

"A farmer went out to sow his seed. As he was scattering the seed, some fell along the path, and the

birds came and ate it up. Some fell on rocky places, where it did not have much soil. It sprang up quickly because the soil was shallow. But when the sun came up, the plants were scorched, and they withered because they had no root. Other seed fell among thorns, which grew up and choked the plants. Still other seed fell on good soil, where it produced a crop—a hundred, sixty or thirty times what was sown. He who has ears, let him hear...

...Listen then to what the parable of the sower means: When anyone hears the message about the kingdom and does not understand it, the evil one comes and snatches away what was in his heart. This is the seed sown along the path. The one who received the seed that fell on rocky places is the man who hears the word and at once receives it with joy. But since he has no root, he lasts only a short time. When trouble or persecution comes because of the word, he quickly falls away. The one who received the seed that fell among the thorns is the man who hears the word, but the worries of this life and the deceitfulness of wealth choke it, making it unfruitful. But the one who received the seed that fell on good soil is the man who hears the word and understands it. He produces a crop, yielding a hundred, sixty or thirty times what was sown."

Matthew 13

I like to think that as broken as I was when I first heard the good news of Jesus' sacrifice for us, that His seed was planted so deep in one of the tears in my soul, it could never be stolen. Maybe the more broken we are, the better, in order to truly receive and hold on to the seed that brings about our eternal life.

To change the direction of our lives, and get to the wonderful place God created for us, we have to start by *replacing* the words in our heads. If we replace the words in our minds with the word of God, and water His seed within us instead, true transformation takes place.

But as we saw in Jesus' parable, it is not easy to hold on to that word as we go through this life. People throughout history made so many sacrifices and endured countless hardships, and many lost their lives, so that we might have the freedom and the ability to hear the word of God and know the truths in the Bible. By ignoring it, or making light of its importance, we take all of their efforts for granted.

"All scripture is God-breathed and is useful for teaching, rebuking, correcting and training in righteousness, so that the man of God may be thoroughly equipped for every good work."
2 Timothy 3:16

Through the Bible's many translations – originally written in Hebrew, then translated to Greek, then to Old English, and finally to modern English – much of the richness and symbolism and the meanings of the chosen words and names in the Bible have been diluted. But with the aid of the Holy Spirit to reveal the true meanings of the original writer's intent, the words and the truth are as rich as they were when they were originally inspired by God.

So why is the "word of God" in the Bible so important?

If you think about it, there is not a minute or even one second during the hours of the day in which we are awake that words are not running through our minds. Whether you are having a conversation with someone out loud, composing one in your head, or rehearsing a conversation you will be having later, words are at all times streaming through your mind. Whether you are listening to the television or to song lyrics, or you are reading, there is a constant river of words flowing through your mind.

Can you hear the stream of words in your head? Try to stop them. Were you able to do so, or did another word creep in? Even when we try to clear our minds to meditate, we have to focus on another word like "Ohmmmmm."

It is impossible to halt the stream of words. We can only hope, with all of our efforts, to reduce the stream to a single word at a time. In this level of consciousness, in this stream of consciousness, words are always present. It is only when we are in the deepest stages of sleep – or under anesthesia, for example, existing in another level of consciousness – that only the essence of the words are present. The energy is there but it doesn't manifest itself in word form. It is all potential. It exists in the form of its superposition we spoke of earlier, hovering in God's realm only known to Him.

"Before a word is on my tongue you know it completely, O Lord."
Psalm 139: 4

More on that notion to come, but for now let's start at the beginning.

"In the beginning was the Word, and the Word was with God, and the Word was God."
John 1:1

Our Creator created everything we see with words. He "spoke" the entire universe that visually manifested itself into existence.

From Genesis 1:
"In the beginning God created the heavens and the earth. Now the earth was formless and empty, darkness was over the surface of the deep, and the Spirit of God was hovering over the waters. And God *said*, 'Let there be light,' and there was light."

So much of the mystery of our universe could be better understood if we understood the roots of our language. In the original Hebrew language (in fact, even within every letter of the Hebrew alphabet) the story of how our universe was created, and how all things relate to each other, can be learned.

As a quick example, if we look at the meanings of the word "origin" and the word "oral," both have the same Latin root "or" – meaning "from the mouth" and "to appear." (God originated all things orally.)

In the same way God created with His words, we (who are made in His image) also create with our words. Anything that we have built or brought into this world first began with the words we spoke either out loud or in our minds. Words become material. The word of God is the beginning of it all. And it is the also the end.

"Heaven and Earth will pass away, but my words will never pass away."
Matthew 24:34

That quote is from Jesus himself as He explains the self-fulfilling, ideo-dynamic response, and the inevitable outcome designed and built into the meaning of all words.

Words accomplish what their intents are. They never return void or empty. They never return without having altered or affected someone or something.

"So is my word that goes out from my mouth: It will not return to me empty."
Isaiah 55:11

Words are received, conceptualized and materialized everywhere.

The sounds and the meanings of a word in your mind can literally change your entire body chemistry. With functional MRI's, scientist can actually see brain activity lighting up in different areas of the brain as different words are introduced. [4]   Dr. Brian Pasley of the Helen Wills Neuroscience Institute suggests in his recent paper that the patterns in brainwave activity upon hearing different sounds may allow researches to one day construct the actual words that are forming in the subject's mind without them having to speak, thus allowing stroke victims to communicate for example. Pasley predicts that with technological advances, we will be able to know what words are on a person's mind simply by looking at the energy patterns in their brain images! [5] (Remember this later when we talk about a word being on your forehead.)

And as we saw with the experiment by Dr. Emoto, the unseen energy vibrations of these words not only create specific brain activity, but they can even affect the molecular structure of the world around us.

In addition, when we pair words with a melody they resonate in our minds with even greater strength. Song lyrics in particular are easily remembered even decades after hearing them due to the associations made in our brains with the music behind them. Knowing this, it is no wonder that Satan attempts to keep his words ruminating in our minds by pairing some of the most hate-filled, violent words with music. While some songs may seem benign, the words in them can fester in your mind and literally alter your moods, behaviors and actions, again leading you down the destructive path he wants you on. If God's words could be set to music, they too would resonate longer in our minds and create the outcome they intend instead.

"Speak to one another with psalms, hymns and spiritual songs..." Ephesians 5:19

"From time immemorial, sound and music have been associated with creation – or primary vibration – of the universe itself. In the East, the Mahabharata epic of India explains that out of the ineffable One came the symmetrical and numerical variations that underlie physical structures. In China, the *I Ching*, or *Book of Changes*, reflects a similar harmonic understanding. In the West, the Gospel tells us that in the beginning was the Word." [6] -*The Mozart Effect*, by Don Campbell.

In addition to Campbell's observations about the universality of music, we have recently been introduced to the "string theory." We will talk more about this later when we touch on quantum mechanics.

For now, as the Mozart effect suggests, consider that the melodic sounds in music resemble what we were enveloped in before we were born – both in the womb and in the place of our Creator, from which He created us and where He resides. This is the same place from where His breath creates the vibration that shapes our souls and the song of the entire universe around us. What a beautiful orchestra it must be for one to be able to hear all of the sounds of the universe in harmony together. We are only able to hear a tiny, tiny fraction of the sound energy waves that are produced by all things. Having spent time in many magnetic resonance imaging (MRI) machines over the last few years, I had the opportunity to experience what magnetic forces sound like. In their normal levels, our human ears cannot hear them, but when concentrated – as they are in the high powered MRI machines – they are astoundingly loud. When we think of how the entire universe operates with electro-magnetic forces, I can't help but wonder what a beautiful sound it must be to the One who created it all.

"At this my heart pounds and leaps from its place. Listen. Listen to the roar of his voice, to the rumbling that comes from his mouth. He unleashes his lightning beneath the whole heaven and sends it to the ends of the earth. After that comes the sound of his roar; he thunders with his majestic voice. When his voice resounds, he holds nothing back. God's voice thunders in marvelous ways; he does great things beyond our understanding." Job 37

Humans all over the globe, regardless of their cultures, have attempted to recreate the familiar sounds of music. Our brains are born wired already for these memories.

"Music helps plants grow, it soothes, resurrects, and transforms." As Campbell says, "It is the primal breath of creation itself, the speech of angels and atoms, the stuff of which life and dreams, souls and stars, are ultimately fashioned." [7]

In the same way we recognize the sound of music, our spirits also recognize the true words of God. With or without music, His words will resonate within our souls just like music to our ears. The truth feels recognizable like nothing else. From where our spirits came, in the dimension of God, full of love and truth, we recognize these things when we feel them here. We are born already wired with them in our hearts and minds.

"This is the covenant I will make with them after that time, says the Lord. I will put my laws in their hearts, and I will write them on their minds."
Hebrews 10:16

In Genesis, we see what Biblical scholars refer to as the fall of man. The perfect state of Earth fell when original sin produced its first fruit. This is why what we see today is such a poor reflection of what God's true words spoke our world into. The changes occurred when the evil force upon the earth twisted God's word for the first time. Until that point, life was without sickness or death, it was perfect and effortless. The truth of God simply took its shape in our material world. Our DNA was harmonious and perfect. Our cells were perfect and flawless, living simply by following the instructions they were given by God Himself as He spoke us into this realm.

"As for God, his way is perfect; the word of the Lord is flawless."
2 Samuel 22:31

But at the time of the first sin, Satan took the words that God had given to Eve and twisted them. He essentially said to the woman, "Did God *really* say 'You must not eat from any tree in the garden?'" – causing her to doubt God's word. By this same spirit, most of us are full of doubt and unbelief still today.

So, now is the time to stop doubting God's perfect word. He is the Creator, and His plans for us are perfect and good.

It is only by twisting, or distorting, or by using words falsely, that the enemy of God has any ability. The devil cannot create words. Unable to create anything himself, he can only twist words to cause us to doubt the truth of God's words, in order to alienate us from God and to carry out his will instead.

From the very first time he spoke into Eve's mind, through generations and generations, he has simply been twisting God's words to destroy rather than build. Then he cleverly gets his twisted thoughts into the minds of individuals who speak his lies to others, who in turn believe them and act on them, destroying their lives, and the lives of their believers. And the cycle of pain, suffering and abuse continues. For years I watched in dismay as a "friend" of mine spoke poorly to his friends about their spouses. And then I watched as their relationships became slowly broken and ultimately ended in divorces. If only they had recognized my "friend's" remarks for what they were. Who was my friend planting seeds for?

"When he lies, he speaks his native language for he is a liar and the father of lies."
John 8:44

With your words you can either build a person up, or tear him down. You can encourage and strengthen or discourage and destroy.

"With the tongue we praise our Lord and Father, and with it we curse men, who have been made in God's likeness. Out of the same mouth come praise and cursing. My brothers this should not be. Can both fresh water and salt water flow from the same spring?"
James 3:9

As James talked about our words coming from streams of either salt water of fresh water, we have to be careful to watch which energy source *our* words come from. Without the Spirit of God in us, the words *we* speak are most likely coming from the twisted energy of the world. They are just empty with no truth in them. As the Bible also warns us: **"Let no one deceive you with empty words." Ephesians 5:6.**

Don't forget that although it was the devil who spoke the first lie, Eve first chose to believe it over what God had said. She, in a sense, handed over her trust from God to Satan. And since then, we have been witnessing the world becoming more and more visually distorted by our collective continued belief in his lies.

God's words meant for one thing to appear, and yet we believe the distorted reflection of that light energy instead. Satan was originally described as a fallen angel covered in shiny mirrors that reflected God's light. It makes sense, then, that by this same means he deflects the true intention of God's spoken energy so that it manifests visibly in our world, shy of perfection.

This is the grand illusion some refer to. It is why what we now all see is merely the distortion of the perfect design God spoke into existence. We see our fallen world, riddled with illness and disease, genes gone awry, wars, division, hunger, pain, fear – none of these being the intention of our Creator, and all of these being the result of the manifestations of our beliefs in the twisted lies of Satan.

"Now we see but a poor reflection as in a mirror, then we shall see face to face."
1 Corinthians 13:12

We find ourselves now in a world that has been so infiltrated over thousands of years with the twisted lies of the evil one, that it often seems difficult to discern what words and thoughts are from God and what has been a lie carried down through generations, adopted as the truth by popular culture.

But God says:

"Who told you that you were naked?"
Genesis 3:11

After eating from the forbidden fruit in the Garden of Eden, Adam and Eve look at themselves shamefully and run off to hide from the Lord, telling Him, "We hid from you because we are naked." Just as Eve became led to believe in the twisted version of the truth as told to her by the serpent, after incorporating and believing the twisted associations we've been shown, we also think something must be wrong with us. We don't look like the pictures in the magazines. Our lives don't resemble those portrayed in the movies. So like Adam and Eve, we also hide in our shame. (Our dissonance has become the driving force behind many consumer related industries.)

But God sees us for the truth and beauty that we are, and He asks *this* of Adam and Eve: "Who told you that you were naked?" (Where did these lies come from, that have led you to hide from me," He asks.) We need to ask ourselves the same thing. Who says *this* is what love looks like? Who says this is what is beautiful?

The point is we need to listen to what we are being told. Is there dissonance within us when we hear it? Does it not match God's word that is hidden inside us? Remember the cognitive dissonance we spoke about earlier.

In **1 Thessalonians 5:21** God's word says to "**Test everything.**" The things we are told that go against God's word will create cognitive dissonance within us.

But, if it is the truth, there will be *resonance*.

Even though our minds can at times be easily deceived, our souls, belonging to God, know the truth.

Because we are born from truth, our spirits recognize it (if we let them listen). God's pure truth will resonate and be recognized from within, in the same way that the strings of a musical instrument vibrate together if they are tuned to the same note.

"He who belongs to God hears what God says."

In the same way infants are soothed and healed by the melodic sounds of classical music that resemble the familiar sounds and rhythms they were used to in the womb, we also are soothed and healed by the sound of the true words of God.

"For the word of God is living and active. Sharper than any double edged sword, it penetrates even to dividing soul and spirit, joints and marrow; it judges the thoughts and attitudes of the heart."   Hebrews 4:12

Since the world is a dark, distorted mirage at this point, the true, untwisted word of God becomes like a sword penetrating the darkness and letting the true light seep in.

The truth can cut like a knife, freeing us from the hold of lies over our lives. As we recognize it more and more and let it resonate within us, incorporating the true word of God into our lives, we become in tune and in harmony with the creative power of the universe, in harmony with our Creator.

And the more adept we become at recognizing the truth, the better we are able to recognize what God's perfect plan for us and our lives really is. Similarly, I once read that although children of broken, hurting families face reality in ways that were not designed by God, they still know in their hearts the way things should be. [8]

"In the same way, the Spirit helps us in our weakness. We do not know what we ought to pray for, but the Spirit himself intercedes for us with groans that words cannot express."

Romans 8:26

"He calls his own sheep by name and leads them out. When he has brought out all his own, he goes on ahead of them, and his sheep follow him because they know his voice."
John 10:3

Are you only hearing the words of the world, or can you hear the true voice of God?

By slowing down our breathing, pulse rate and metabolism, and by allowing our basic physiological state to be at rest from the world long enough, we can reach the place of stillness, of quietness. Here in this state our souls are better able to listen and hear, and to receive the word of God.

Science reveals to us the release of endorphins and other positive chemicals that take place when we tune in to the thoughts of God. It is here, where our bodies and minds are at rest, where we stop wanting for ourselves and where the energy of the word of God can do its best healing work.

"Be still, and know I am God."
Psalm 46:10

Or, as my precious daughter says when she notices I'm acting on unnecessary stress, **"Calm thyself."**

When we let go of our efforts and of ourselves – of our very "person" – we can stop and listen for God's voice, allowing it to speak its true design to all of our cells, transforming us into who He created us to be.

As James also tells us, our lives are but a mist that lasts a short time.

> **"What is your life? You are a mist that appears for a little while then vanishes."**
> **James 4:14**

With that said, it makes sense that the word "person" comes from the Greek and Latin roots "per" and "son," meaning "the sound passes through." 9

But imagine if we no longer listened to the voice of the enemy, and only the words of God were allowed in our minds and in our bodies. We would grow to the healthiest state of being, and our destiny would be that of eternal life with God.

The word "unison" comes from the prefix "uni," meaning "one," and the root word "son," which as we just learned, means "sound."

Unison = One Sound.

At a certain time we will all be healed, made whole, and shaped into the likeness of Christ. We will then be more than just a person and a "mist" – we will have become a part of the everlasting God. We will be in unison through the one Son, all resonating with the same sound. (More on this sound to come…)

But as we stay tangled here in our collective belief of lies, we witness instead a world of suffering and death.

Although our illnesses and ailments were never intended, over milenniums of collectively believing and acting on untruths, they have manifested. Our beliefs and behaviors parted from how God created them, and now our continued rebellion has allowed them to stay.

The truth is that God will still continue to use these things for His grander plan, for the good of those who love Him and are called to His purpose. He can use anything for our ultimate good. And eventually the truth of an entirely different, perfect world, where none of these illnesses exist, will come to fruition. We will collectively get back to this perfect place at the appointed time.

"Do two walk together unless they have agreed to do so?"
Amos 3:3

I love how Freeda Bowers puts it in her book, *Give Me 40 Days of Healing*: No matter what our ailments are, they exist because we have come under the agreement with them that they are the truth, that they are real. 10

God's word says:
"Again I tell you that if two of you on earth agree about anything you ask for, it will be done for you by my Father in heaven."
Matthew 18:19

Look for like-minded people who rather than walking around with the words of the world in their minds, walk with the Holy Spirit, to speak the truth that you are whole and you are perfect, you are healed and you are loved. Stand in agreement with one another in God's words.

Interestingly, the word "health" comes from the Old English word "hal," a root word signifying whole, healing, and inhaling. And the word "heal" in Northern Middle

English means "to make sound, to become healthy again." 11 —from *The Mozart Effect*.

As we lie still, we can remember the root definition for the word *health*: "inhaling"; and for the word *heal*: "to make sound." And then breathe in the Holy Spirit, and let it heal you. Then let the sound of God's words resonate in you.

Listen to the word of God:
"I tell you the truth, if you have faith as small as a mustard seed, you can say to this mountain, 'Move from here to there' and it will move. Nothing will be impossible for you."
Matthew 17:20

It's time for all of us to wake up from the subconscious entanglements we are led by and break free from the distraction and the allure of popular culture, and to recognize the power of the words in our minds.

We talked earlier about what it is in us that subconsciously drives us to behave and act, what is leading us from within. Now we *know* that it all begins with a word.

Just like a seed that eventually grows to produce a fruit, a word will take root and grow to produce its result. It reminds me of a time I was somewhat able to see this occur firsthand. After talking one morning about a milkshake with a friend, the word grew in his mind. By the end of that day, sure enough he had gone out to buy one.

So now we can recognize that allowing a word in our minds enables it to develop. And eventually, that word gets acted on. Knowing this, we can hopefully recognize when we are acting on lies coming from twisted words within us, or on the truth.

"Now that you have purified yourselves by obeying the truth so that you have sincere love for your brothers, love one another deeply, from the heart. For you have been born again, not of perishable seed, but of imperishable, through the living and enduring word of God."   1 Peter 1:22

"Therefore, get rid of all moral filth and the evil that is so prevalent and humbly accept the word planted in you, which can save you. Do not merely listen to the word, and so deceive yourselves. Do what it says."
James 1:21

8

- The Real Secret -

Having understood all of this, I'm going to go a little bit deeper still and reveal now that it is not just God's word that needs to be in our minds to truly make any changes in our lives. Here is the real secret: It is God Himself.

"And the word was God."
John 1

Yes. The word is God. It is the essence and the energy of God from which words originate.

Please keep reading…

"For the word of God is living and active."
Hebrews 4:12

We have been alluding to this concept in earlier chapters, and now you might be thinking, "What? Words are energy, 'living and active'?" If this seems confusing, hopefully sharing the experience I had when I first heard God "speak" will make it clearer.

I had set out in search of God. There were things going on in my life that had me riddled with fears and anxieties and I had no idea what I should do. I needed to hear from God.

I was worried about what one person was going to think of me if I made one choice, or what others would think if I did another thing. I was overwhelmingly confused and frustrated and scared. I was even considering moving so I could just run away and not have to deal with any of the challenging decisions I faced. Or, I thought maybe I could take a stand.

But what if this person was angry if I made one choice? Or that person was upset if I made another? Ugh! I was tortured over what was the right thing to do.

Thankfully, at that point in my life I had already come to believe that the living God truly existed, so I set out in search of Him so He could show me what decision to make. I went outside for a walk, filled with emotions, distraught over these choices and the reactions and judgments of the people they would affect. Faced with not knowing what the right thing to do was, I sat down on a bank of grass by a small lake near my house and cried out to Him in my mind's words.

I poured out my heart. What should I do? Should I say this to this person, that to another? What will they think? What will—?

Then God interrupted me with a giant *BOOM*. His voice shook me to my core and left me silent. Then it instantaneously filled me with overwhelming gratitude that brought me to tears. What He said was not at all what I was expecting. I thought God would tell me which choice was right and what I should do in that situation.

But instead, what He said was even better. What He powerfully interrupted my chatter with was four distinct words: "**None. Of. It. Matters.**"

I literally felt His words with their powerful essence – their energy.

Later, as I thought about sharing this experience with a friend, I contemplated how I would explain this occurrence. I thought about the questions she would ask me, and I also wanted to know the answers myself.

One of the biggest questions I figured she would ask in disbelief was: "So, the God of the entire Universe speaks in English?" I spent some time thinking about this and tried to understand how this experience actually took place.

I eventually realized what had happened. When the energy of His words had come down to me, I heard and *felt* them, and my mind had instantly translated them into English.

If you stop to think about it, this is the way we all receive information. For example, when we take in the visible energy of light waves through the lenses in our eyes and recognize the shape of a chair, our brains instantly form the word "chair" to match what was perceived. When we recognize the vibrations of the sound waves of a ringing bell, we've learned to call that particular dynamic pattern of sound waves a "bell." When we feel the energy from within our bodies as chemicals associated with the emotion of happiness are released, the word our mind uses to sum up this energy is "happy." Or when our brains perceive the energy of love, it registers as the English word "love." It is the language everything has been associated with for those of us who have grown up speaking English. If I had grown up translating the world around me into Spanish, my mind would have translated the meaning of God's spoken energy into its Spanish equivalent.

But having learned the world in English, when I felt the energy of God's words, they were instantly translated to: *"None of it matters."*

We will talk more about the meaning of that powerful message God gave me that day. But for now, remember that our brains process billions of bits of information every second, from within and outside of our bodies. All of this information comes in different forms of energy.

So we now understand that it is energy, in various forms, that make up the essence of the words in our minds. The actual words themselves are just our minds' translations of the energy we perceive.

My Pastor has spoken in church lately about the root words "logos" and "rhema," both Greek words meaning "word." The appearance of both of these words in the original Greek version of the New Testament is making people stop to think about the multiple forms that a "word" can be used. 1

Some people think the word "logos" is used to describe the complete, fully manifested form of the word, such as when it becomes apparent in writing. And that "rhema" is used to describe the spoken form of the word.

Similarly, in English we have one word for snow, while the language of colder, northern countries may have multiple words that all mean some variation of "snow," such as "wetter snow" and "slowly falling snow."

The English word for "word" is obviously not enough to fully describe the multiple facets that make up a word. Just like our word for snow doesn't quite cover all of the forms and variations of types of snow.

One of the variations of the word "word" that we do not really have any English word to describe is the form of a word as it comes in its energy or its essence, prior to being translated – its spiritual form.

It is by this unnamed form of the word that the disciples were said to be able to speak to a large group of people from various different cultures (all knowing different languages), and yet have the entire crowd understand the words they were saying, even though they were all understanding them in their own native language.

The disciples were somehow speaking the energy of the words. They were speaking in spirit.

"When they heard this sound, a crowd came together in bewilderment, because each one heard them speaking in his own language."
Acts 2:6

As we go a little deeper, we will see that it is of the essence of God, it is His Holy Spirit that speaks His true words to us. And that it is from His dimension, His heavenly realm where *all* energy originates in infinite possibilities.

It is from here that all words are shaped, enter our world, and become a part of our conscious awareness. Energy is released from God's dimension into ours. Then our brains, which have been trained to translate what they perceive from all of our senses, translate those perceptions into words. The essence of that energy as it is released from the Creator becomes the outcome that we observe (as we discussed earlier.)

Notice again in Genesis: First God spoke, and *then* the things He said appeared. But prior to their manifestation, the vibration, or the energy of God, hovered all around His creation. It all began with the sound – the vibration of God being all around, in all places. And then His intent when He spoke altered the tune, the pitch, and the frequency of the vibrations He emitted, and the exact manifestation of the frequency of His intent became visible.

Maybe this is why the first sensory organ to develop in the womb is the ear (before the eyes). Because what exists is "heard" before it is seen. Since we know that light travels at a faster speed than sound, it must be that the sound is already present in all things if it is to be detected first. According to the "string theory," every quantum particle actually exists in the shape of a string with the same vibrating characteristic of the strings of musical instruments. In which case, if every quantum particle that makes up every particle within every atom of everything in the universe is in a sense humming, this would be true. The sound is already there, whenever anything comes to its visual manifestation.

This all present sound within us and around us we will see later is actually the "word" of God.

Existing first in a form of energy, God's words become imparted and manifested into their visual form wherever an observer 'observes' them.

To explain this phenomenon better, we can examine another study describing the science behind it. In 2007, another set of physicists also observed in photons the concept of superposition.

As we learned earlier, in the quantum world, particles such as photons spend most of their existence in a condition called a superposition, meaning the particles exist all around in several possible states at once. What these scientists observed was that the superposition of the particle collapses into one of its states *only* when the particle is observed or recognized by the observer that is present.

It sounds crazy, but these scientists all reported that it is the belief of the observer that determines where that particle should go, in conjunction with the intended destination of the particle that determines the final state in which the particle will materialize.

Physicist Serge Haroche and his team at Ecole Normale Superieure in Paris reported that they were able to watch the process and the collapse of this superposition as it occurred in a single photon. Again, they witnessed a single particle of light existing in this superposition, then instantly manifesting itself in the state of being where it was ultimately observed. 2

As we noted earlier, the Copenhagen understanding of quantum mechanics further explains that *all* particles exist in the state of a wave of potential energy which collapses into its particle state when it is measured.

Offshoots of this theory also maintain that both states actually exist at the same time, in a phenomenon called wave/particle duality. These scientists all agree that the energy materializes only exactly where and when it is observed. And as we will see more, the when and where of how it is observed is affected by the beliefs of the observers.

When God speaks, He simply moves energy in our dimension. His quantum particles – which exist in infinite places, hovering all around –in forms we can see (light energy) and even more so in forms we cannot see (dark energy) can instantly manifest whenever He determines. And because they exist everywhere in their superposition, they can be rearranged and manifested into their particle state wherever He deems it (and we believe it).

This energy can manifest anywhere. As we will see, Jesus can bring all things into the light so to speak.

More on that to follow, but for now, just know that if it is His intention, the already available energy will manifest where He deems it. In the case of words, it will manifest as waves of energy we can sense in our minds, recognized or observed through our senses as a word.

"The Spirit gives life; the flesh counts for nothing. The words I have spoken to you are spirit and they are life."
John 6:63

"The solidity of our world seems indisputable, yet quantum physics has proved that our physical reality is nothing but a very elaborate mirage. A super-hologram of information. A matrix..." [4]

All physical matter is the result of particles vibrating at a certain frequency.

And everything has its own particular vibration frequency that differentiates itself. This is true of the energy of matter and the energy of words. As we noted earlier, every word and every name vibrates with its own natural frequency, allowing us to differentiate one from another, and allowing it to carry out its intention.

"This is what we speak, not in words taught us by human wisdom, but in words taught by the spirit, expressing spiritual truths in spiritual words."
1 Corinthians 2:13

"The heavens declare the glory of God...
There is no speech or language where their voice is not heard. Their voice goes out into all the earth, their words to the end of the world."
Psalm 19

The Face of God 138

9

- The Word is Jesus -

"The word became flesh and made his dwelling among us."
John 1:14

As we just noted in Haroche's experiment, the quantum particle existed in a superposition until it materialized where and when it was observed. With this concept we saw the need for an observer to agree in belief that where the particle manifested is where the particle should go. So the experimenter himself seemed to play a role in the collapse of the superposition. [1]

It is a widely held belief among physicists today that "human observation of a microscopic event changes the reality of the event." – Bohr and Heisenberg. [2]

Just as with the laws of physics, where the beliefs of observers affect the outcome of events, so too do our beliefs affect everything we see. Our beliefs work hand-in-hand with the beliefs of others at every moment, readjusting accordingly and instantaneously. It is an ever-changing matrix, where one belief forever alters another, which in turn changes the matrix again. In an attempt to demonstrate the math behind this, scientists developed an experiment, where two observers, referred to as *Alice* and *Bob*, independently measured the direction of the "spin" on a pair of electrons as they existed in what was called their "spin singlet" state.

Although their measurements were recorded independently, it became apparent that once Alice measured the spin as going in one direction (along the x-axis), Bob's simultaneous measurement of the spin *always* indicated it was going in the opposite direction. However, immediately *preceding* Alice's measurements, Bob's outcomes could have only been determined statistically. What this means is that the results of Alice's measurements appear to have traveled from Alice to Bob instantaneously, thus resulting in Bob's set measurements. Particle physicists explain this as an effect of entanglement- that our views, beliefs, observations, etcetera are entangled, (to put it very simply.) Interestingly, "Experimental results have demonstrated that effects due to entanglement travel at least thousands of times faster than the speed of light."[3]

In other words, we are *not* independently "measuring" the world around us. My reality is *not* independent of yours. Your "measurement" of the physical world, or your beliefs, will instantaneously affect how the world is "measured" through my perception as well. And the same is true of mine to yours, just as Alice's seemed to play a role in determining Bob's.

In essence, in the same manner that the butterfly effect functions, where every action we take physically alters the world around us with a ripple effect, so too does this principle work with our beliefs. The instant we believe something to be, the world is also physically altered by that belief.

"Again I tell you that if two of you on earth agree about anything you ask for, it will be done for you by my Father in heaven."
Matthew 18:19

It is not surprising, then, that the search for the elusive "God particle" has yet to allow scientists to observe its presence. When God determines it is the right time, and we all believe it, then we will not only be able to see its effects, but the particle itself. But just like the photon reflects the awesome essence of God's light, and this Higgs boson particle (the 'God particle') reflects the unifying omnipresence of Christ, we need to remember when we see it, that the real thing is still to come. **"The law is only a shadow of the good things that are coming- not the realities themselves." Hebrews 10:1**

As a Christian these experiments may make you stop to wonder though, *When will this happen?* and *Is it free will or is it God's will at work in the world?*

The answer is sort of both; all things will come together at the exact right time, when God sees fit *and* when we believe.

According to Jesus as He explains this to His disciples, **"Where there is a carcass, there the vultures gather." (Matthew 24:28)**

We constantly witness examples of apparent "divine appointments," when what we deem to be either our individual or our collective free will seems to intersect with God's predetermined plan, at the exact appointed time.

In scripture we are shown several examples of this through Christ and His disciples. Many times they seemed to have chosen not to perform a miracle, or they would be selective about who could be present at the time of the healing. Altering the physical world would at times, it seems, requires the collective belief that the alteration could occur. As one example:

> "In Joppa there was a disciple named Tabitha, which when translated is Dorcas, who was always doing good and helping the poor. About that time she became sick and died, and her body was washed and placed in an upstairs room. Lydda was near Joppa; so when the disciples heard that Peter was in Lydda, they sent two men to him and urged him, Please come at once." Peter went with them, and when he arrived he was taken upstairs to the room. All the widows stood around him, crying and showing him the robes and other clothing that Dorcas had made while she was still with them. Peter sent them all out of the room, and then he got down on his knees and prayed. Turning toward the dead woman, he said, 'Tabitha, get up.' She opened her eyes, and seeing Peter she sat up. He took her by the hand and helped her to her feet. Then he called the believers and the widows and presented her to them alive."
> **Acts 9:36**

Peter knew that with others in the room the observed outcome of his prayer may have been altered by their unbelief, so he dismissed the room first before praying. Then, with only his belief and the agreement of God's will to answer his prayer, her state of being changed from dead to alive by both observers, Peter, and God. On her feet again, Tabitha was presented alive to the others.

Similar stories of healing occur throughout the Bible, each time with the explanation from Christ that it is by the faith, or belief, of the one who is healed that they were saved. If the person did not believe that Christ and God could heal them, they would not have been healed. Scientists refer to this phenomenon as the placebo effect. In essence, if a person believes a drug of some sort will help him, it does. Others call this the power of mind over matter.

It is this effect, in conjunction with the dependency witnessed in the spin measurement demonstration between Alice and Bob that explains how our collective belief creates our physical reality.

However, as questioned by many by the creators of the documentary *What The Bleep Do We Know,* 4 if we think for a moment about the current manifestation of all of the particles in our universe that exist in their collapsed state, things seem to remain in place even when we, as the observers, look away. But since we now know that the nature of all quantum particles is to exist in a potential wave-like state before manifesting where they are observed, only to take on their particle state in the moment that this observation or measurement takes place, then why do the physical manifestations stay in place when we are not observing them? Or along those lines, how is it that a particle takes its shape in the remote jungle where there is no actual observer to create the collapse of its superposition?

The answer is Jesus.

There exists an "overall observer." It is this omnipresent observer who holds all things in their place, when we as human observers aren't there to measure or observe them for ourselves.

Max Planck, a German physicist and one of the founders of quantum theory, said that "all matter originates and exists only by virtue of a force which brings the particles of an atom to vibration which holds the atom together. We must assume behind this force is the existence of a conscious and intelligent mind. This mind is the matrix of all matter." 5

The apostle Paul answered that question for us two thousand years ago, when he explained that in Christ all things hold together:

"For by him all things were created: things in heaven and on earth, visible and invisible, whether thrones or powers or rulers or authorities; all things were created by him and for him. He is before all things, and in him all things hold together."
Colossians 1:16

"In the beginning was the Word, and the Word was with God, and the Word was God. He was with God in the beginning.
Through him all things were made; without him nothing was made that has been made..."
John 1:1

"The Son is the radiance of God's glory and the exact representation of his being, sustaining all things by his powerful word."
Hebrews 1:3

We have learned that the word is God. And now we can see hidden in scripture that the manifestation of God that is described as the "word" or as the "seed" that was with God in the beginning is actually Jesus Christ. He is the seed that is the word. He is the force that holds all things together. It is by *His* energy we are transformed and saved. He was the "word that became flesh." It is His same Spirit that works in our minds and our bodies to accomplish His will. He is the "gateway to heaven." He is the "bread of life," He is the "one true vine," and He is the "shepherd for our souls," and the cornerstone by which the entire kingdom of God is built.

He tore through the fabric of the universe to lead us to God. It is *His* energy that we need to be transformed by and into. At the last day, we need to be hidden in, or covered by, the energy of Christ.

His name is the one word with all the power.

"In the last days, God says, I will pour out my Spirit on all people. Your sons and daughters will prophesy, your young men will see visions, your old men will dream dreams. Even on my servants, both men and women, I will pour out my Spirit in those days, and they will prophesy. I will show wonders in heaven above and signs on the earth, below, blood and fire and billows of smoke. The sun will be turned to darkness and the moon to blood before the coming of the great and glorious day of the Lord. And everyone who calls on the name of the Lord will be saved."
Acts 2:21

"The Lord will be king over the whole earth. On that day there will be one LORD, and his name the only name."
Zechariah 14:9

"...and his name is the Word of God."
Revelations 19:31

He is the one Son, the one sound through which we all resonate in unison.

It has been made well known by the lecture series "How Great is Our God" that the proteins in each of our cells, whose function is to hold all of our cells together like glue, are called laminins. As we know, proteins and peptides take on a myriad of shapes and sizes, each one unique to its function. These unifying proteins that are found throughout each and every one of our microscopic cells, which are responsible for holding all our cells together, exist in the shape of microscopic crosses. As they work all day long, holding life together without even a hint of our conscious awareness of them, we can see the repetition from the micro scale to the macro scale once again as hidden confirmation to us of the great design of life itself by our Creator. 6

"For you created my inmost being; you knit me together in my mother's womb."
Psalm 139:13

"Let the word of Christ dwell in you richly..."
Colossians 3:16

"By the power of your name, the name you have given me."
John 17:11

"On hearing this, they were baptized into the name of the Lord Jesus."
Acts 19:5

"...in order that the love you have for me may be in them and that I myself may be in them."

John 17:26

The word becomes the thoughts that become the intentions that become the actions that create the habits that form our character. Our character determines who we are and who we become: our destiny. So, what if the word in you was Jesus? It would follow that your destiny would be the same as His: eternal life.

Okay, now we are getting there. This is the key. Here is the crux of it all: In the end, those who have been transformed throughout every cell in their bodies into the same energy as Jesus Christ will become enveloped and lifted up with God's energy, becoming a member of the Kingdom of Heaven. No other name carries the same vibration frequency. This is the name, the word we need feeding our cells and to be "covering" us with its energy. This is why we are told to focus on Jesus.

"For you died, and your life is now hidden with Christ in God. When Christ, who is your life, appears, then you also will appear with him in glory."
Colossians 3:1

"Salvation is found in no one else, for there is not other name under heaven given to men by which we must be saved." Acts 4:12

Because Christ overcame everything, even death, as He rose on the third day, He is clearly able to have authority over all things. He has the power to break all strongholds. He submitted Himself to every form of suffering imaginable to break *every* cycle of the physical realm. For our sake He did this, allowing us to be freed from the cycles we are enslaved to as well.

His ultimate sacrifice frees us from our past. And His life was a model for us to follow. He was the master of breaking cycles even as He walked in human form. As He explained:

"But I tell you who hear me: Love your enemies, do good to those who hate you, bless those who curse you, pray for those who mistreat you. If someone strikes you on one cheek, turn to him also the other..." Luke 6:27

"When they hurled insults at him, he did not retaliate; when he suffered, he made no threats. Instead, he entrusted himself to him who judges justly."
1 Peter 2: 23

As we better understand the fullness and sovereignty of God, and the way in which He created the entire universe to operate, this becomes easier and easier for us to do – that is, we learn that we do not have to retaliate or seek revenge.

"God is just: He will pay back trouble to those who trouble you and give relief to those who are troubled."
2 Thessalonians 1:6

Whether you want it to happen or not, this is one of the laws of the universe: cause and effect, karma, or whatever you want to call it. And we are under this law. We, too, will be paid back for our wrong doings; we will suffer the consequences of our sins – *unless* we take hold of the accomplishment of Christ.

The only way out of the trappings of the fabric of the universe we are in is through the work of Christ. It is only by belief and faith in the work He has already done for us that we are saved. Only then, embracing what Jesus accomplished and by allowing His spirit to lead our new lives, are we freed from our consequences of our past and connected to the source of life and love abundant, no longer under the law, but covered in grace.

"So do not think that I have come to abolish the law or the Prophets: I have not come to abolish them but to fulfill them. I tell you the truth: until heaven and Earth disappear, not the smallest letter, not the least stroke of a pen, will by any means disappear from the Law, until everything is accomplished."
Matthew 5:18

At the time of Christ's return, all things will make sense and transform into a meaningful relationship as we discover how everything has fit together perfectly for the ultimate fulfillment of God's redemption plan, headed by Him. At that point the whole order of things, the past laws we knew, the concepts, the struggles, the world and its desires will in an instant be changed for us all.

Until the time that all of this occurs, we can personally become freed and receive this promise, connecting ourselves to God's redeemed plan by our own personal choice to repent and be baptized.

"Repent and be baptized, every one of you, in the name of Jesus Christ for the forgiveness of your sins. And you will receive the Holy Spirit. The promise is for

you and your children and for all who are far off – for all whom the Lord out God will call."
Acts 2:28

It is this one name: Jesus Christ.

No other energy frequency is the same. *This* is the energy that baptizes and fills us. The energy of Him – the part of His triune nature called His Holy Spirit – given in His name. This is the only always available, freely given, holy and perfect energy that our every cell can feed on and become addicted to – the only energy source that leads us to life. Any other chemical energy frequency will not. It is the energy of His Holy Spirit in you that can *replace* all other chemicals or toxins, that can wash your every cell making it pure and holy and well, transforming your future from within. Any other frequency is false, and will not save you. All others will just distract, and disguise, and keep you trapped in their cycles. But by His path, in the frequency of His name, we are saved

"Make every effort to enter through the narrow door, because many, I tell you, will try to enter and will not be able to. Once the owner of the house gets up and closes the door, you will stand outside knocking and pleading, 'Sir, open the door for us.' But he will answer, 'I don't know you or where you come from.'"
Luke 13:24

"Do not be amazed at this, for a time is coming when all who are in their graves will hear his voice and come out- those who have done good will rise to live, and those who have done evil will rise to be condemned."
John 5:28

The *only* path to fully overcoming the world and all of its lures, so that you can be among those who will rise to truly live, is through Jesus.

"Whoever believes and is baptized will be saved, but whoever does not believe will be condemned."
Mark 16:16

"Who is it that overcomes the world? Only he who believes that Jesus is the Son of God."
1 John 5:5

Yes, He is that significant. All of the prophesies before Christ pointed ahead to Him, and now all of the science after His death points back to Him. This might be why in the laws of physics, created by God, there seems to be no difference in the ability of time to systemically affect and alter the physical realm both forward and backward. [7]

Scientists are still baffled by these concepts. Physicist Yakir Aharanov of Chapman University recently submitted his take on this by saying, "What is really happening in the double-slit experiment, and really wherever atomic particles are interacting with each other (that is to say, everywhere), is not that the two electrons are in two places at once. Instead, time is running both forward, from the electron leaving the wire, and backward, from its final location on the second screen. Where time meets, running backwards and forwards, determines which slit the electron chooses. The future is affecting the past, all the time, on the quantum level." [8]

I think his theory is very interesting. Should it prove to be true, these two scriptures will have been explained to me by it.

"I tell you the truth, whoever hears my word and believes Him who sent me has eternal life and will not be condemned; he has crossed over from death to life." John 5:24

"For we are God's workmanship, created in Christ Jesus to do good works, which God prepared in advance for us to do." Ephesians 2:10

Once we have made the choice to believe Jesus, our final destination changes from death to life. Working backward then, our final landing place would aid in determining which doors we walk through in the same way that the final landing spot on the detection screen aided in determining which slit the electron would pass through as well.

Just like the loop feedback cycle of our mental processes has shown us, the final goal or destination does aid in determining our every choice along the way (consciously and on a subconscious level.)

For me, most of these concepts can be somewhat represented by a zipper. The entire zipper exists the whole way through, from bottom to top. But it has two sides that either stay apart or come together perfectly along the way up. One side could represent the material, visual world, while the other is the reality that God has already planned. And the fastener in the middle is Christ. As we ride along with Him, we can see what God has already planned from start to finish come together with what we see, hear, touch, and manifest in the material realm.

"I am the Alpha and the Omega, the First and the Last, the Beginning and the End." Revelation 22:13

"If anyone is to go into captivity, into captivity he will go. If anyone is to be killed with the sword, with the sword he will be killed." Revelation 13:10

10

- Clothe Yourself -

"You are all sons of God through faith in Christ Jesus, for all of you who were baptized into Christ have clothed yourselves with Christ."
Galatians 3:26

Over and over in the Bible, we are told to become hidden in Christ, to "clothe" ourselves with Christ, to clothe ourselves with the characteristics of Christ – with love and healing and compassion. We are told to follow His example, to overcome the world, washing our every cell clean from the world and covering them instead with the holiness and righteousness of Christ. Why is this so important?

As we know, the human body is made up of various chemical compounds, including water, carbohydrates in various forms, amino acids that form proteins, nucleic acids that form DNA and RNA, etcetera. These compounds in turn are all made up of elements such as carbon, hydrogen, oxygen, nitrogen, iron, zinc, and so on.

All of these chemical compounds and elements occur in various forms and combinations throughout the entire universe. *Again,* it is simply these same 118 elements combined in different ways that are the building blocks of everything in our entire universe including our bodies.

We now know all of these elements are simply made up of atoms. These atoms are made up of the same particles – protons, electrons and neutrons. The only thing different from an atom of one element and an atom of another element is the number of these particles the atom contains. I know we have said all this before, but I really want us to see how easy it is for God to change *everything*.

Every atom of one element contains the same amount of protons and electrons, which differs in number from any other element. So, for example, put in simple terms, potassium atoms all contain 19 protons and 19 electrons. But, if someone were to add one tiny little proton and one tiny little electron to a potassium atom, it would no longer be potassium, it would be calcium! If one proton and one electron were added to every atom in a container of potassium, the entire container would be changed to calcium.

As we have learned from the laws of the universe so far, what is true on a microscopic scale is also always true on a larger macroscopic field. The entire universe operates on the same principles. So to witness something at work in the microscopic arena means the same could be witnessed somehow on a larger scale. In the same way our bodies break down and metabolize our food, rearranging and assimilating molecules for different purposes, for example, so too does God with the body of Christ and with all of His creation.

With that said, we should take note of what has been termed the "photoelectric effect."

When an electron absorbs energy from electromagnetic radiation of a very short wavelength (such as ultraviolet light), its increase in energy allows it to be ejected from the atom it had revolved in. Electrons emitted like this are called photoelectrons. This phenomenon was first observed by Heinrich Hertz in 1887 and became known for a while as the "Hertz effect." In order to create a freed photoelectron, the activating light source needs to be of a certain frequency. Einstein explained this further by postulating that only photons of a high enough frequency, above a certain threshold value, could knock an electron free. In his demonstrations, for example, a photon of blue light had sufficient energy of the right frequency to knock an electron free of metal, but one of red light did not. [1]

So, in other words, photons vibrating at the *right* frequency can knock electrons free of the atoms they had been a part of. When an atom loses an electron, it becomes electrically charged and available to bond in a different molecular structure. (Hopefully, we can recall this from high school chemistry class – that chemical compounds are created by ways in which electrically charged atoms bond to create molecules with other electrically charged atoms.)

So from this we can see that a tiny wave of little photons, with the right frequency introduced to a system, can alter that system's molecular structure. Earlier we learned that the photon is the smallest particle of light that still retains all of the properties of light. We noted that light is of the same energy as God. "God is light," as we are told many times in scripture. Jesus is the light of the world.

Thanks to John Iannone and others, many of us have been made aware of the awesome phenomenon that revealed itself in the Shroud of Turin, believed by most scientists to be the burial cloth of Jesus Christ. A mysterious image of a man was somehow imparted onto the cloth. The possibility of it having been painted on was ruled out in the labs. This is something that has never been witnessed on a burial cloth before or since. Within the last century, a photographer who was developing images he shot of the cloth discovered that on the negative (or reverse image) of his films, the actual image of Christ had emerged. In the same way that light creates a photograph by first imprinting a 'negative' image on the back of the film in a camera, the imprint of Christ's body was literally ingrained onto the cloth by the powerful light He emitted at the time of His resurrection! 2

"God is light." (1 John 1:5)

By the same principle that allows a photon, (the smallest particle of light) at a certain wavelength to knock an electron free from its atom, so too can the energy of God move entire molecules, changing the chemical compounds and the resulting material world we observe.

After multiplying a few loaves of bread and fish to feed thousands, Jesus sails away on a boat and further demonstrates His power to change the molecular structure of materialized things by walking on the surface of the water. Days later, He multiplies bread again to feed another four thousand people. He gets on another boat to sail off with His disciples. Moments later, as the disciples are arguing about how little bread they now have to eat, Jesus says to them:

"Why are you talking about having no bread? Do you still not see or understand? Are your hearts hardened? Do you have eyes but fail to see, and ears but fail to hear?"
Mark 8:17

As we learned earlier, the protons and electrons that make up all of the atoms that are materialized in our world are made up of multiple quantum particles. And we learned that quantum particles are like waves of energy that exist in infinite states, until those quantum particles manifest in our material world as determined by the will of the overall observer. They exist all around in their potential form, just waiting to be spoken into this realm into the protons or electrons or neutrons that God intends for them to become.

In our galaxy alone it appears that there exists 10 times more unmanifested energy than that of the quantum particles that *have* been spoken into our visible realm. Yet, of those particles which have already manifested, even they exist both in their collapsed particle state and as waves of energy at the same time, held in their manifested state only by the omnipresent observance of the triune God.

How easy it must be for God to change the material elements we see just by allowing a few of his quantum particles into our dimension! With the simple transfer of energy by one word, God creates life here. With one breath, He can send billions of quantum particles into their collapsed state wherever He intends, altering the molecular structure of our entire universe. On the day Christ reappears, we are told that he will completely destroy the evil one simply by the power of His breath and the splendor of His coming.

"...And then the lawless one will be revealed, whom the Lord Jesus will overthrow with the breath of his mouth and destroy by the splendor of his coming." 2Thessalonians2:8

Jesus re-entering our realm in full form! Wow!

Everything we have talked about up to this point has been to prepare us for this day. If nothing else in this book sticks, let it be this next part. What we are going to witness is that the energy of God's presence in our realm will change everything. And for those interested in being a part of the kingdom of heaven, what we are "wearing" at that time will determine our destination. Being clothed in Christ will be the key to receiving the energy we need to make the leap into the everlasting life with Him. The science behind this will explain further.

"Then you will know the truth and the truth shall set you free."
John 8:32

In the early 1900's, when the discoveries in quantum mechanics were being made, they appeared to violate the most basic of laws we had believed to be true in physics:

- *The principle of space and time*, i.e., physical objects (systems) exist separately in space and time in such a way that they are localizable and countable, and physical processes (the evolution of systems) take place in space and time;
- *The principle of causality*, i.e., every event has a cause;
- *The principle of determination*, i.e., every later state of a system is uniquely determined by any earlier state;
- *The principle of continuity*, i.e., all processes exhibiting a difference between the initial and the final state have to go through every intervening state; and finally...
- *The principle of the conservation of energy*, i.e., the energy of a closed system can be transformed into various forms but is never gained, lost or destroyed.

(From http://plato.stanford.edu/entries/qm-copenhagen 3)

2000 years prior, when Christ's miracles were being witnessed, they too appeared to violate the very laws of the world.

As this has been explained in scripture, once you believe in Jesus…

…you are not under law, but under grace."
Romans 6:14

At work in the universe, underneath the laws of physics, has always been the underlying workings of quantum mechanics. And at work in the universe underlying our physical world has always been the underlying work of the spiritual world which Jesus patiently attempted to show us.

As scientists discover more and more about the chemistry behind our emotions, our thoughts, and all of the functions of our bodies, we have to remain aware that underlying all of these chemicals are quantum waves of energy, and that it is God's will that determines where that energy will go.

We saw earlier that Jesus is the one overall observer that dictates where waves of energy materialize in their particle state, and by His omnipresence, keeps them held together. Jesus himself healed and reshaped material things when He walked in His human body, but everything He did was only in accordance with God's will.

"I tell you the truth, the Son can do nothing by himself; he can only do what he sees his Father doing, because whatever the Father does the Son also does."
John 5:19

It is all God's will – all of it. In the experiment we spoke about earlier with Alice and Bob, which was conducted to demonstrate the simultaneous effect of one belief instantaneously determining the reality of the other, we saw that it was Alice who measured the "spin" first, and that Bob's measurement was simultaneously determined by hers. If this demonstration could be used to explain our relationship to the Creator, He would always be the "Alice," while we are all always "Bobs." His divine plan is *that* encompassing. There is nothing we can do which God does not allow. And a vast portion of our brains were designed to worship Him with this awareness and reverence – that we are one with Him, integral parts of His awesome creation, created to do good works which He prepared in advance for us to do.

"I form the light and create the darkness, I bring prosperity and create disaster; I, the Lord do all these things...

...Woe to him who quarrels with his Master." **Isaiah 45:9**

"The creation waits in eager expectation for the sons of God to be revealed. For the creation was subjected to frustration, not by its own choice, but by the will of the one who subjected it, in hope that the creation itself will be liberated from its bondage to decay and brought into the glorious freedom of the children of God." **Romans 8:20**

It is difficult from where we observe to comprehend this complete sovereignty of God. Also difficult to embrace is the seeming duality of God – His left hand of judgment and His right hand of grace. And yet He is fully sovereign and He embodies both judgment *and* grace. Similarly, His quantum particles exist as both waves (like the always available grace of God) and as particles (having collapsed into their materialized state as the judgment of God manifests). The work of Louis de Broglie verified this phenomenon not only for elementary particles, but also for compound particles like atoms and even molecules. In fact, "according to traditional formulations of non-relativistic quantum mechanics, wave-particle duality applies to all objects, even macroscopic ones; but because of their small wavelengths, the wave properties of macroscopic objects cannot be detected." [4] He is sovereign over all things from the microcosm to the macrocosm.

Christ's examples of healings – and, in fact, everything He did – was in accordance with God's plan, a plan that supersedes all aspects of life from large to small, from the future to the past. And as we learn new quantum principles, we need to remember that they too are working in accordance with His plan, which Jesus demonstrated with His life and in His teachings. For example, consider what Jesus demonstrated when he turned a jug full of hydrogen and oxygen atoms (water) into wine. We can also now imagine what happens when a priest or a pastor (who truly believes) blesses the communion elements. Even further, as we ingest these elements, Jesus tells us to think of these as His body and blood that He gave up for us.

We have seen how real and consuming our thoughts are, how they affect every cell and molecule in our bodies, how they can literally alter the molecular structure of physical things, and how they shape our intentions, which then create our actions, altering the physical world around us.

Jesus said, **"Do this in remembrance of me."**

Imagine praying over our food and drink, thinking the thoughts of Christ, and then ingesting them, breaking them down to their molecular level through the digestive process, where our thoughts and beliefs can alter their very molecular structure, changing them into the energy of Christ Himself, to be distributed through our bloodstream, to then be fed to our every cell. As internationally-renowned psychopharmacologist Dr. Candace Pert explains it, our blood cells rush in during the digestive process to receive the converted energy from our foods, and carry away the new peptides back to all of the parts of the body to heal and restore and complete their assignments. 5 Are the peptides your body is producing perfect, holy and life renewing? Or are we further covering our cells with the peptides associated with the broken emotions of the world?

"Do not call anything impure that God has made clean." Acts 10:15

Jesus said to them, 'I tell you the truth, unless you eat the flesh of the Son of Man and drink his blood, you have no life in you. Whoever eats my flesh and drinks my blood has eternal life, and I will raise him up at the last day.'"

John 6:53

This is a difficult concept to grasp, but imagine how Jesus' followers must have felt (with no knowledge at that time of quantum particles or of the nature of these particles), when Jesus spoke so metaphysically to them. In fact, on hearing this, "...**many of his disciples said, 'This is a hard teaching. Who can accept it?'"**

Then Jesus attempts to explain to them that He is speaking in spiritual concepts and spiritual truths.

"The words I have spoken to you are spirit and they are life. Yet there are some of you who do not believe... this is why I told you that no one can come to me unless the Father has enabled him."
John 6:63

Faith is a gift from God. Even now, with more knowledge of the subatomic world and the spiritual energy Jesus was describing, we still have a hard time accepting this. It helped me to consider further the physiological concepts brought to light by Pavlov that we discussed earlier.

As we eat, we create strong associations in our brains between the foods and the chemicals of the thoughts in our bodies. This is one of the reasons why people often eat out of loneliness, boredom, depression, or whatever else to which they have chemically linked the action. But the apostle Paul explained that we should examine ourselves beforehand, and correct our thoughts, acknowledging the Lord, and judging ourselves so that we will not be condemned with the world. (1 Corinthians 11:31)

If we could change our thoughts to be focused on Christ with every communion, His energy would be linked with the act of eating and drinking. Just as in the reality of Pavlov's dogs, if we pair the stimuli or energy of Christ with the food that gives our cells their energy, and then repeat these pairings over and over, eventually the middle stimuli can be removed and the energy of Christ would be what provides the energy that fuels our bodies.

The cells in our bodies replicate themselves at the rate specified by their DNA. They also are "instructed" to adjust or evolve according to what their surroundings are. They adapt to survive on what they are being fed. As we saw earlier, each generation of new cells will have more openings to fit the peptides in the proteins of the chemicals they have been fed, and fewer openings for other things, including the nutrients from our foods. 6 This is what aging is all about – each generation of cells learns how it needs to be shaped according to what it is being fed. What if we broke the cycle every time and fed our cells with the natural frequency they were designed to live on? We would see a reversal in aging, as the cells throughout our body would grow to conform to the way they were perfectly designed. Jesus in a sense is the "fountain of youth." Or better yet, as He explained to us:

"I am the living bread... If anyone eats of this bread, he will live forever." John 6

He truly would be the "bread of life."

Please remember we are still speaking in terms of quantum physics and spiritual concepts.

But, with these concepts in mind, we are beginning to see how following Christ's commands begins to change our physical bodies on a cellular level. In addition, we can now add to that consumption, the change in our thoughts when we allow the Holy Spirit to fill us, and we become further transformed in our thinking, until a point when our cells are completely "covered" by the Holy Spirit.

Remember that antacid tablet we talked about and how it covered every molecule in the water? Picture that again as you read these next few scriptures and hear how we are being told the way to prepare for the last day, the day of Christ's return:

Jesus said to them, **"I tell you the truth, unless you eat the flesh of the Son of Man and drink his blood, you have no life in you. Whoever eats my flesh and drinks my blood has eternal life, and I will raise him up at the last day."**
John 6:53

"And do this, understanding the present time, the hour has come for you to wake up from your slumber, because our salvation is nearer now than when we first believed. The night is nearly over; the day is almost here. So let us put aside the deeds of darkness and put on the armor of light. Let us behave decently, as in the daytime, not in orgies and drunkenness, not in sexual immorality and debauchery, not in dissension and jealously. Rather, *clothe yourselves* **with the Lord Jesus Christ, and do not think about how to gratify the desires of the sinful nature."**
Romans 13:8

"Blessed are those who wash their robes, that they may have the right to the tree of life."
Revelation 22:12

"Behold, I come like a thief. Blessed is he who stays awake and keeps *his clothes* **with him, so that he may not go naked and be shamefully exposed."**
Revelation 16:15

"They will walk with me dressed in white, for they are worthy. He who overcomes will, like them, be dressed in white."
Revelation 3:4

Interestingly, the root word used in Hebrew for the word atonement is "kaphar," which means "to cover." [7]

So again, why is this important? Why do we need to be washed clean, covered, and clothed in the holiness of Christ? Why did John set an example for us by baptizing in water, and Jesus set an example for us by washing his disciples feet?

Listen to the word of God:

"I declare to you, brothers, that flesh and blood cannot inherit the kingdom of God, nor does the perishable inherit the imperishable.

"Listen, I tell you a mystery: We will not all sleep, but we will all be changed -- in a flash, in the twinkling of an eye, at the last trumpet.

"For the trumpet will sound, the dead will be raised imperishable, and we will be changed. For the perishable must clothe itself with the imperishable, and the mortal with immortality. When the perishable has been *clothed* with the imperishable, and the mortal with immortality, then the saying that is written will come true: "Death has been swallowed up in victory."

1 Corinthians 15:50.

A time is coming when all of God's children will be enveloped by God. Metaphysically speaking, having overcome the world and having been transformed into the likeness of Jesus, upon His return, our now completely washed spiritual bodies will be lifted up and gathered into Christ to live for eternity in heaven.

"For as I have often told you before and now say again even with tears, many live as enemies of the cross of Christ. Their destiny is destruction, their god is their stomach, and their glory is their shame. Their mind is on earthly things. But our citizenship is in heaven. And we eagerly await a Savior from there, the Lord Jesus Christ, who, by the power that enables him to bring everything under his control, will transform our lowly bodies so that they will be like his glorious body."
Philippians 3:18

Again, as mentioned earlier, every cell in our bodies needs to be sanctified, washed clean of the toxins produced by the thoughts and the actions of the world. Every cell needs to be covered and clothed with the chemical energy that radiates from the love that is God and His Holy Spirit.

Previously I wrote about the words being made up of sounds all containing the frequency of the vibration that carries the meaning behind them.

And we talked about how the various energies of words are perceived by our minds and translated for us into whatever language we have come to learn the world around us in. We learned that God is the breather of the entire plan of the Universe, and that His word which is in, around, and throughout everything, holds all things in place.

We learned that it is the word, the name of Jesus Christ, which carries all of the power of the Creator behind it. And it is this name with all of His attributes we are told to be "clothed" in. Once all of our cells are covered in the vibration of His name, tuned to and resonating at the same energy frequency, miracles happen.

And finally, it is at the time of Christ's return to our physical realm that it is necessary for us to be clothed in *His* frequency.

At that time, with His trumpet call, all those vibrating or "oscillating" at the same wavelength frequency as *Him* will be imparted with his burst of energy and transformed completely into our spiritual eternal forms.

"For the Lord himself will come down from heaven, with a loud command, with the voice of the archangel and with the trumpet call of God, and the dead in Christ will rise first. After that we who are still alive and are left will be caught up together with them in the clouds to meet the Lord in the air. And so we will be with the Lord forever."
1 Thessalonians 4:16

I have to admit, this concept was a stumbling block for me. I just couldn't accept it on faith alone. I needed something I could wrap my brain around that might help me truly believe what scripture is saying.

So God, in His understanding grace for my lack of faith, once again shared the science behind it with me by introducing me to a few more of His designs, including "resonators," "resonant energy transfer," and "quantum tunneling."

"Let the word of Christ dwell in you richly..."
Colossians 3:16

The Face of God 170

11

- On That Day -

"This is what the Lord Almighty says: 'In a little while I will once more shake the heavens and the earth, the sea and the dry land. I will shake all nations, and the desired of all nations will come, and I will fill this house with glory,' says the Lord Almighty."
Haggai 2:6

When a note is plucked or strummed on a stringed instrument, it vibrates in such a way that all other nearby strings which are tuned to the same note – or frequency – begin to vibrate as well. This is a phenomenon called "resonant energy transfer," which can be defined as the transfer of energy between two fields or two systems that are highly resonant at the same frequency. [1]

As we learned earlier, *all* things in creation are vibrating in waves of energy at certain frequencies.

In physics, resonance is considered to be the tendency of an object or a system to vibrate with larger amplitudes at a particular frequency. The frequency allowing for the largest oscillations within the system is called its natural, or resonant, frequency. When a system is operating on its natural or resonant frequency, even a small driving force can produce progressively larger oscillations within the system because all systems store vibrational energy, often referred to as potential energy. We learned earlier that before forming the heavens and the earth, God hovered all around, as do waves of sound. And then when He spoke, He altered the frequency of His voice, uttering a command: "Let there be light." From there, He continued speaking the universe into its visual existence, giving all things in creation the vibrational energy of His voice within them. Our natural frequency is the one that matches the frequency of His voice as He spoke us into existence. I will explain this further.

First, note what occurred in Nikola Tesla's experiment. We now know that resonance occurs as a system oscillates or vibrates with larger and larger amplitudes; as it becomes further fueled by the introduction of another system that is operating on its same particular frequency – its resonant frequency. Remember in his experiment that depending on the frequency of the vibrations he tuned the vibrator to, different objects in the room, and throughout the city, would vibrate. When he changed the frequency of the device, different objects which were naturally oscillating on that same frequency would also start to shake. He caused miniature earthquakes by simply adding a small amount of vibrating energy to the naturally occurring vibrations of different objects! This concept is so important that God created all systems to operate this way.

"Resonance occurs in all types of waves and vibrations. There's the acoustic resonance as we mentioned, there's mechanical resonance, electromagnetic resonance, nuclear resonance, electron spin resonance and resonance of quantum wave functions, etc. And, all systems with resonance can be affected by the resonant energy transfer from a resonator." 2

When Nikola Tesla first witnessed this phenomenon, he knew he was on to something huge. But without knowing God's word in the Bible, he wasn't able to recognize what the real significance he felt was all about.

But now, by God's grace, we can! Having learned about the Word of the Lord existing as energy, vibrating at its own distinct frequency, which we can sense at times when we are most open to it, we are now able to recognize that it is when we are aligned with the frequency of God's word that our systems become supplied with the energy that He imparts.

It is through this physical change in our systems, as we come to oscillate with our resonant frequency (the natural frequency we were designed by our Creator to operate on, - that of the same frequency of Christ), that we begin to enjoy the gift of His energy working in our lives. It is by growing into our natural resonant frequency that His pre-spoken plan unfolds, allowing us to ride the wave of His energy flow.

"My grace is sufficient for you, for my power is made perfect in weakness."
2 Corinthians 12:9

Earlier I shared the experiences I had while recovering from heart failure, when the only way I was able to muster enough energy to work was by praying and by functioning through the motivating energy of love. And as we know, Jesus is love. I was flowing with the same wavelength and frequency as God's natural design of love for us, instead of working against it.

In this world though, it is easy to allow other words, thoughts, and "dampening frequencies" to interfere with our natural frequency.

"*Natural frequency* is the frequency at which a system naturally vibrates once it has been set into motion. In other words, natural frequency is the number of times a system will oscillate (move back and forth) between its original position and its displaced position, if there is no outside interference." 3

"Therefore ... let us throw off everything that hinders and the sin that so easily entangles. And let us run with perseverance the race marked out for us. Let us fix our eyes on Jesus..."
Hebrews 12:1

When God set the universe in motion, it had within its design all the laws and the commandments of God. Christ explains the greatest commandments of all:

"Love the Lord your God with all your heart and with all your soul and with all your mind and with all your strength. The second is this: Love your neighbor as yourself." Mark 12:30

There is no fear in love. But perfect love drives out fear... (1 John 4:18)

Clearing our hearts of our own selfish ambitions and instead opening up to God to fill us with His Spirit of love will allow us to operate from a place of love, travelling on the easiest path with no resistance. It is our natural frequency.

"And now these three remain: faith, hope and love. But the greatest of these is love."
1 Corinthians 13:13

"Do everything in love." 1 Corinthians 16:14

It is here, when we have surrendered our will to His greater will, allowing His word to grow within us, and with Him guiding our lives, we begin to see that in Him we can accomplish all things.

"I can do all everything through Him who gives me strength." Philippians 4:13

As Jesus has said, "With God, all things are possible." When we trust and believe God, working with His energy and will, rather than the multitude of varied frequencies we could succumb to, we are no longer "kicking against the goads."

"Saul, Saul, why do you persecute me? It is hard to kick against the goads."
Acts 26:14

This metaphor comes from a Greek proverb explaining useless resistance – as the ox in the proverb succeeds only in hurting itself. 4

However, when our wills are aligned with God's, we can ask anything in Jesus' name – in love and all of the attributes of Christ – and it will be done. I once heard a Pastor say: "We fit just how He created us." Not trying to be more than what we are, just doing everything we do for the glory of Him who made us a perfect part of His design, like perfectly tuned instruments in His glorious symphony.

Another way to think of it is like this: Picture a swing oscillating back and forth. As you are pushing a child on the swing, you notice that if you add your force at just the right time in the already formed momentum of the swing in motion, you will make it go higher and higher. But if you are off in timing, you will actually be working against the forces already in motion and the energy flow of that swing will be dampened, and the swing will not oscillate as high. 5 It is the same concept with us and God. As we become aligned with His already spoken plan, with the forces He has already put into motion, we get to enjoy the streams of energy moving us effortlessly forward as we follow His will and His energy flowing from His word within us.

"Whoever believes in me, as the Scripture has said, streams of living water will flow from within him."
John 7:38

But our efforts against the flow of God's pre-spoken plan will be futile and will die out, just as the oscillation of the swing will continue to be dampened and eventually come to a stop if we continue to push against the forces already at work in its motion.

"If you remain in me and my words remain in you, ask whatever you wish, and it will be given you. This is to my Father's glory."
John 15:7

It is by allowing God's energy to resonate within us that we can move mountains.

In order to receive the "resonant energy transfer" from our ever-present God, we need to be vibrating or oscillating within every cell at the same frequency as His.

When another system is introduced to a system that is already operating on the same wavelength, a phenomenon called "resonant energy transfer" occurs. Energy becomes transferred from one system to the other, thus allowing the additional energy that is already stored in the second system to be transferred from its potential form to its kinetic form. At that point, operating in its natural resonant frequency (if there aren't any dampening energies working against that system), the energy oscillations within that second system will skyrocket in exponential proportions!

"Have faith in God." Jesus answered. "I tell you the truth, if anyone says to this mountain, 'Go, throw yourself into the sea,' and does not doubt in his heart but believes that what he says will happen, it will be done for him." Mark 11:22

Not surprisingly, the system or entity that imparts its vibration energy to others with the same frequency is called a "resonator." Manmade devices called resonators are used in different ways in the world "to either generate waves of specific frequencies, or to select out specific frequencies from a more complex signal containing many frequencies." [6]

Musical instruments use resonators to produce sound waves of specific tones. Homogenous systems that are also tuned to the same frequency as these tones will actually

The Face of God 177

receive the energy from the resonator and this energy will be added to their system. We can see this happening in strings of a guitar as the vibration of one will cause the other to also vibrate when tuned to the same note. One of the most recognizable manmade resonators today is the tuning fork. Operating on this same principle, it emits a pure tone, transferring its energy to the strings or chords that are tuned to the same pure note.

It is very interesting to learn from the founder of the string theory that every single tiny microscopic quantum particle that makes up everything we know of in the entire universe is also shaped like a string – vibrating to the natural frequency that its Creator tuned it to.

The Universe truly is an orchestra of sound.

So why is it important for us to now note this God designed phenomenon? Why does any prophet make his revelations known? Why does God allow us to learn anything? The answer to these is always the same- for our future. It is always to help us, protect us, or guide us in future events that the ability of learning and remembering anything exists. And, in the case of this knowledge of resonant energy transfer, it is the same: for the sake of our future. This phenomenon has been revealed to prepare us for the day of Christ's return. The Bible speaks of the last day of the world as we know it as the day Christ comes with His "winnowing fork" to separate the wheat and the chaff.

"He will baptize you with the Holy Spirit and with fire. His <u>winnowing fork</u> in his hand to clear the

threshing floor and to gather the wheat into his barn, but he will burn up the chaff with unquenchable fire."
Luke 3:17

As we know from Jesus' parable about the farmer, the wheat represents those who have allowed the seed of God to grow within them, thus transforming them into the frequency of Christ; the chaff are the ones who are grown from the seed sown by the devil (Matthew 13:24).

The Holy Spirit led me to research what is a 'winnowing fork?' It was then that it clicked. God's example in scripture of this two pronged device called a 'winnowing fork' that He will use to draw up his wheat on the last day looks just like a two pronged tuning fork! It is a resonator.

God is telling us to be prepared in our whole system to be able to receive the resonant energy Christ's powerful presence will impart so we don't miss out on our opportunity to be a part of His gathering.

Those who have been transformed into the likeness of God, having been baptized and having allowed the Holy Spirit to dwell in them where every cell in their body is covered with the same frequency as the energy of God will be imparted with this final blow of energy resonating powerfully from Christ in order to be gathered to Him. And those who rejected Him and never repented, who are still entangled and clothed in the energy and chemical makeup of the world, will be left behind for the final condemnation of the earth as we know it.

As we saw earlier, with this incredible resonant energy being transferred (and without any dampening energy to stop the momentum of the receiving system), the energy of that system oscillates at larger and larger amplitudes, becomes exponentially greater and greater and quickly produces another phenomenon called 'tunneling.'

As an example, in quantum mechanics, "quantum tunneling" is the phenomenon where a particle *tunnels* through a barrier that it usually could not surmount because its total mechanical energy is normally lower than the potential energy of the barrier. However, with the resonant energy transferred to it, the total mechanical energy of that particle becomes exponentially enhanced, allowing it to break through. And on the day of our Lord, the energy imparted to those souls who are covered in the same frequency as His name will enable a *leap* through the barrier that has been separating us from God for so long.

"Surely the day is coming; it will burn like a furnace... Not a root or a branch will be left to them. But for you who revere my name, the sun of righteousness will rise with healing in its wings. And you will go out and *leap* like calves released from the stall."
Malachi 4:1

"Then the lame will leap like a deer." Isaiah 35:6

When John the Baptist was conceived, an angel of the Lord first appeared to his father and said:

"Don't be afraid, Zechariah; your prayer has been heard. Your wife Elizabeth will bear you a son.... And he will be filled with the Holy Spirit even from birth."
Luke 1:11

A few months later an angel told Mary that the son of God was to be conceived in her by the Holy Spirit – we all know this story. But what we may not remember from this chapter is that even when the baby Jesus was in His mother's womb, He was still able to impart His resonant energy. And as soon as the little one in Elizabeth's womb (who had been sanctified by God and set apart for His purpose, therefore vibrating at the same frequency) came near the presence of God, he was imparted with a burst of energy.

When Elizabeth heard Mary's greeting, the baby *leaped* in her womb and she was filled with the Holy Spirit. Luke 1:41

Upon nearing the proximity of Christ (while still in His mother's womb) and hearing the sound of His mother's voice, John received the resonant energy from Jesus and *leaped*, even in the womb.

For me, resonant energy transfer and quantum tunneling explain the science behind how we will be "gathered" to Him, as this next verse describes:

"For the Lord himself will come down from heaven, with a loud command, with the voice of the archangel and with the trumpet call of God, and the dead in Christ will rise first. After that we who are still alive and are left will be caught up together with them in the clouds to meet the Lord in the air. And so we will be with the Lord forever."
1 Thessalonians 4:16

"Once more I will shake not only the earth but also the heavens. The words 'once more' indicate the removing of what can be shaken -- that is, created things- so that what cannot be shaken may remain, Therefore, since we are receiving a kingdom that cannot be shaken, let us be thankful, and so worship God, acceptably with reverence and awe, for our God is a consuming fire."

Hebrews 12:26

God has told us. Over two thousand years ago, this was written. With the winnowing fork and the trumpet call as symbols of resonators to accomplish the transfer of Christ's energy to ours on the day He returns.

Just as in Tesla's study, on that day the whole earth will shake, with all vibrations at their peak of intensity. We saw a small glimpse of this power with the loud trumpet declaring God's presence at Mount Sinai when the entire mountain shook as He spoke the commandments to Moses.

In Exodus 19, it says that the sound of the trumpet grew louder and louder. Then the voice of God spoke to Moses: **"Go down and warn the people, even the priests, who approach the Lord must consecrate themselves or the Lord will break out against them."**

Again we see the need to consecrate, or by definition to sanctify, to make holy, to set apart ourselves for a particular purpose. - *(dictionary.com)* 7

To be prepared for this day we need to repent and receive atonement (to put this in religious terms).

From Merriam Webster:

Repent: to turn from sin and dedicate oneself to the amendment of one's life.

Atonement: the reconciliation of God and humankind through the sacrificial death of Jesus Christ. 8

God is telling us again of the importance of ridding ourselves of the toxins of the world and setting aside our lives for Christ. Repeatedly (for those of us who are stubborn) we are told this consecrating, this overcoming of the world, needs to take place so we are not dampened or entangled, so we can be covered with Christ, allowing us to break free from the physical realm. If not, our ties, addictions, strongholds, cravings, and whatever else is leading us in our earthly nature will keep us here and make us miss the life that we were truly created to be a part of!

On that day no one who is on the roof of his house with his goods inside, should go down to get them. Likewise, no one in the field should go back for anything. Remember Lot's wife! Whoever tries to keep his life will lose it, and whoever loses his life will preserve it.
Luke 17:30

"Since then, you have been raised with Christ, set your hearts on things above, where Christ is seated at the right hand of God. Set your minds on things above, not earthly things. For you died, and your life is now hidden with Christ in God. When Christ, who is your life, appears, then you also will appear with him in glory.

The Face of God 183

"Put to death, therefore, whatever belongs to your earthly nature: sexual immorality, impurity, lust, evil desires, and greed, which is idolatry. Because of these, the wrath of God is coming.

"You used to walk in these ways in the life you once lived. But now you must rid yourselves of all such things as these: anger, rage, malice, slander, and filthy language from your lips. Do not lie to each other, since you have taken off your old self with its practices and have put on the new self, which is being renewed in knowledge in the image of its Creator.

"Here there is no Greek or Jew, circumcised or uncircumcised, barbarian, Scythian, slave or free, but Christ is all, and is in all.

"Therefore, as God's chosen people, holy and dearly loved, clothe yourselves with compassion, kindness, humility, gentleness, and patience. Bear with each other and forgive whatever grievances you may have against one another. Forgive as the Lord forgave you. And over all these virtues put on love, which binds them all together in perfect unity.

"Let the peace of Christ rule in your hearts, since as members of one body you were called to peace. And be thankful. Let the word of Christ dwell in you richly as you teach and admonish one another with all wisdom, and as you sing psalms, hymns, and spiritual songs with gratitude in your hearts to God. And whatever you do, whether in work or deed, do it all in the name of the Lord Jesus, giving thanks to God the Father through him."
Colossians 3

And as we said before, we need to make sure we are listening and obeying the words of God. Our connections to

Him need to be the strongest. His voice should be the most recognizable.

Blessed are those who hear the word of God and obey it. Luke 11:28

"My sheep listen to my voice; I know them and they follow me. I give them eternal life, and they shall never perish; no one can snatch them out of my hand. My Father, who has given them to me, is greater than all, no one can snatch them out of my Father's hand. I and the Father are one."
John 10:27

"I tell you the truth, a time is coming and has now come when the dead will hear the voice of the Son of God and those who hear will live."
John 5:24

Along those same lines, on the day of our Lord everything we are able to "see" in this visual world as we now see it will also be changed in an instant. Another similar phenomenon in light waves caused by resonant energy transfer, called "extraordinary optical transmission," will make this possible.

Extraordinary optical transmission occurs when light energy is able to pass through an object which it normally would not be able to surmount, but with the resonant energy added to the light from another source the light energy can be seen tunneling through the object to be visible on the other side. 9

The Face of God 185

Like the lightning that accompanies Christ's return, the resonant transfer of God's energy into our realm will illuminate all things by allowing the light to pass through its former barriers. Where before the light could not seep through, with the resonant energy God imparts, His light will be seen everywhere, and all things hidden in the darkness will be exposed.

"There is nothing concealed that will not be disclosed, or hidden that will not be made known."
Matthew 10:26

"Nothing in all creation is hidden from God's sight. Everything is uncovered and laid bare before the eyes of him to whom we must give account."
Hebrews 4:12- 13

"Therefore judge nothing before the appointed time; wait till the Lord comes. He will bring to light what is hidden in darkness and will expose the motives of men's hearts."
1 Corinthians 4:5

Again, as we saw earlier, the photons of a light beam have a specific energy determined by their wave frequency.

In the photoemission process, if an electron within a material absorbs the energy from one photon and thus has more energy than what's called the "work function" (the electron binding energy) of the material, it gets ejected. If the photon's energy is too low, the electron will be unable to escape the material. If we increase the intensity of the light beam, we increase the number of photons in the light beam, and thus increase the number of electrons in the material that become excited. But increasing the intensity does not increase the energy that each electron possesses. This is because the energy of the emitted electrons does not depend on the intensity of the incoming light, but only on the energy or frequency of the individual photons. Again, it's not about the intensity of the light, but about the frequency. 10

"Not by might, nor by power, but by my Spirit, says the Lord Almighty."
Zechariah 4:6

And it is by the One frequency that we will become tuned into, clothing ourselves with Christ's love that will allow our souls to be freed at the time of His return.

In their search for the definition of consciousness, scientist have been able to conclude that the particular frequency of the brain waves they have been able to witness determines the level of consciousness in an individual. Long waves of large amplitudes can be seen in unconscious patients, and short waves frequencies are present when a subject is awake. The natural frequency of Christ is the one which will truly "wake us up."

"Wake up, O sleeper, rise from the dead, and Christ will shine on you."
Ephesians 5:14

After understanding a little more about the world of chemistry, subatomic particles, physics, and quantum physics as God has designed every system in the Universe to operate, we can now read these scriptures written over two thousand years ago and finally understand their relevance and significance.

"The Son of Man in his day will be like the lightning which flashes and lights up the sky form one end to the other... Just as it was in the days of Noah, so also will it be in the days of the Son of man. People were eating, drinking, marrying and being given in marriage up to the day Noah entered the ark. Then the flood came and destroyed them all.

"It was the same in the days of Lot. People were eating and drinking, buying and selling, planting and building. But the day Lot left Sodom, fire and sulfur rained down from heaven and destroyed them all.

"It will be just like this on the day the Son of Man is revealed."

Luke 17

"When will this happen and what will be the sign of your coming and of the end of age?"

Jesus answered: "Watch out that no one deceives you. For many will come in my name, claiming, 'I am the Christ,' and will deceive many. You will hear of wars and rumors of wars, but see to it that you are not alarmed. Such things must happen, but the end is still to come. Nation will rise against nation and kingdom against kingdom. There will be famines and earthquakes in various places... there will be great distress, unequaled from the beginning of the world until now – and never to be equaled again... Immediately after the distress of those days 'the sun will be darkened, and the moon will not give its light; the stars will fall from the sky and the heavenly bodies will be shaken.'

"At that time the Son of Man will appear in the sky, and all the nations of the earth will mourn. They will

see the Son of Man coming on the clouds of the sky, with power and great glory. And he will send his angels with a loud trumpet call, and they will gather his elect from the four winds, from one end of the heavens to the other."
Matthew 24

"Do not be amazed at this, for a time is coming when all who are in their graves will hear his voice and come out – those who have done good will rise to live, and those who have done evil will rise to be condemned."
John 5:28

"For in just a little while, He who is coming will come and will not delay. But my righteous one will live by faith."
Hebrews 10:37

12

- Just Believe -

Since World War II, the only acceptable method of proving the efficacy of a new drug has been through the FDA's stringent "double blind, randomized, placebo controlled study." 1 Although the thoughts and concepts in this book may never be proven in such a controlled study, they are nonetheless a part of the scientific process of uncovering and understanding the creation around us.

"Thought experiments" are at the heart of all studies. Today they are used throughout our courts to assess culpability in social and legal contexts. 2

Scientists also use thought experiments when particular physical experiments are impossible to conduct. Carl Gustav Hempel labeled these sorts of experiments "theoretical experiments-in-imagination." One example is Einstein's thought experiment on chasing a light beam. This was an important scientific thought experiment. It could never be actually carried out, but it led to the successful theory of Special Relativity which was then proven by other empirical means. 3 Even with "cold hard science," much of what we "know" is based on what we believe to be true; theories we put together by means of other theories. And yet now we know that our beliefs play a huge role in determining what we will see.

If all of this is tough to wrap your mind around, that's okay. Thankfully, God gave us Jesus. Christ has already done the work for us, and His Spirit continues to work within us to perform the transforming our souls need as we live and grow in our faith in Him every day. Just believe in the good news of Jesus.

"For the message of the cross is foolishness to those who are perishing, but to us who are being saved it is the power of God. For it is written: I will destroy the wisdom of the wise; the intelligence of the intelligent I will frustrate. Where is the wise man? Where is the scholar? Where is the philosopher of this age? Has not God made foolish the wisdom of the world? For since in the wisdom of God the world through its wisdom did not know him, God was pleased to save those who believe." 1 Corinthians 1:18

"Jesus asked him, 'What do you want me to do for you?' 'Lord, I want to see,' he replied. Jesus said to him, 'Receive your sight; your faith has healed you.'" Luke 18:40

When a woman riddled with a bleeding disease was healed instantly after crawling through a crowd just to touch His cloak, Jesus responded: **"Daughter, *your faith* has healed you. Go in peace"** Luke 8:49

Then someone in the crowd called out to Him about another woman in his town who had recently died. Hearing this, Jesus said to him: **"Don't be afraid, *just believe*, and she will be healed."** Luke 8:50

"Have faith in God." Jesus answered. **"I tell you the truth, if anyone says to this mountain, 'Go, throw yourself into the sea,' and does not doubt in his heart but believes that what he says will happen, it will be done for him.**

The Face of God 191

"Therefore I tell you, whatever you ask for in prayer, *believe* that you have received it, and it will be yours. And when you stand praying, if you hold anything against anyone, forgive him, so that your Father in heaven may forgive your sins."
Mark 11:22

What are we praying for? If we ever expect peace in our homes, in our country, or on our planet, then we have to be able to forgive each other just as God has forgiven us. The Bible says the Lord is the judge, and He will pay back trouble to those who have hurt us. It is His to avenge. Harboring resentment or a lack of forgiveness will keep us from wearing the clothes we need to be covered in. Trust that God will not let their deeds go unexposed or unpunished, and let Him deliver you away from them to a place where you can be cleansed and healed.

"Blessed are those who wash their robes, that they may have the right to the tree of life and may go through the gates into the city. Outside are dogs, those who practice magic arts, the sexually immoral, the murderers, the idolaters, and everyone who loves and practices falsehoods."
Revelation 22:14

"Have nothing to do with the fruitless deeds of darkness, but rather expose them... for it is light that makes everything visible." **Ephesians 5:11**

"May God himself, the God of peace, sanctify you through and through. May your whole spirit, soul, and body be kept blameless at the coming of our Lord Jesus

Christ. The one who calls you is faithful and he will do it."

1 Thessalonians 5:23

In John 6:44, Jesus tells us **"No one can come to me unless the Father who sent me draws him, and I will raise him up at the last day."** God has all the power, and His Spirit does all the real work. Our part is to choose to believe and allow His Spirit to be our guide rather than what had previously been leading us. But this is a choice we get to make over and over, with every decision and with every thought.

We are constantly given the choice to trust in God. It is by always choosing to believe and therefore rebuking the authority of the devil that we eventually give back all authority here on Earth to God. And, in so doing, we receive the crown of life that was once given to us by Him, but which we handed over to Satan when we chose to believe his lies. Receiving the return of the crown of life means that we are no longer under the curse that came upon us at the time of the first sin. The earth no longer becomes hard for us to toil. Labor is no longer painful. The original plan of the Garden of Eden is restored; in the Garden of Eden life is effortless as we live openly with God, surrendered completely in our trust for Him. And we get to enjoy the beautiful rest and love of that seventh day, the Sabbath.

When we all do this collectively, or at least when the "critical mass" of us chooses to believe and operate on the frequency of God's Spirit, that is when we will witness the return of Christ that will change life as we know it.

Throughout this book, and throughout all areas of life, we have seen that God has put into place the same systems of operation on a micro-scale as those that are at work on a macro level.

For example, we know that there is a carbon cycle that occurs within the system of every living creature, and that that same cycle is operating on a much larger scale between the earth and its atmosphere. We see particles of light traveling on the most efficient pathway between chlorophyll molecules to reach their destination in the same way we utilize *MapQuest* 4 to provide us with the most efficient travel route to reach our destination. We see quantum particle tunneling just as we will see whole spiritual tunneling. And we see the concept of superposition at work in a single photon in the same way we see the superposition of the divinity and trinity of God.

God's microcosms, in essence, operate on the same principles as his macrocosms. Seemingly common sense at this point, it is just another concentric circle in the interwoven fabric of His awesome creation.

One last phenomenon that I think is relevant to point out in our discussion occurs within the tiny strands of chromosomes in our DNA. And on a macro scale it is how the body of Christ, as we are told in scripture, will be made whole when the prophecies are fulfilled.

In 2007, the Nobel Peace Prize for Physiology or Medicine was awarded for work in gene targeting that utilizes this discovery within our cells called "homologous recombination." 5

Homologous recombination is a type of repair method for our genes in which nucleotide sequences are exchanged between two similar or identical strands of DNA. It is most widely used by all of our cells to accurately repair harmful breaks that occur on both strands of DNA, known as "double-strand breaks." What causes these harmful breaks? Radiation: light waves that are of a particular frequency that are harmful within our bodies. After having read the last chapter, we know what frequency these waves are *not* oscillating on. The wrong frequency of light damages our DNA and can eventually lead to cancer. But by means of homologous recombination, these strands can be healed.

In essence, when a pair of DNA strands has been damaged, another pair that is identical or very similar can assimilate with it, taking on the burden of one of the broken ones. Then, as both pairs have one broken and one healthy strand, all four become healed as a DNA polymerase fills in the breaks to match its healthy brother or sister strand, in a sense gluing it back together, making all four healed and fully functional again. 6

What is important to note in this awesome healing process that scientists have now witnessed in our cells, is that the DNA strands must be *homologous* for this to work. In other words, they must be of the same type, of the same nature.

When Christ returns to our realm, all healing will occur for those who are a part of the kingdom of heaven. Our heavenly bodies will be made perfect. It is by this same principle of homologous recombination in the microscopic world that our spiritual bodies on a grander level will be restored when gathered to Christ. And it is by this same principle that the body of believers here needs to now work together as a whole for the common goal of love and unity under the leadership of Christ.

Remarkably, the word *homologous* is made up of the root words "homo," which means "the same," and "logos," which we now know means "the word."

And, if you've been reading this, you know what the word is. We become *homologous* with one another when we all operate under the "same word."

The word, with all of its essence, in its Spirit form, is "Jesus."

When we read these scriptures, we will see this phenomenon at work...

"...with Christ himself as the chief cornerstone. In him the whole building is joined together and rises to become a holy temple in the Lord. And in him you too are being built together to become a dwelling in which God lives by his Spirit."
Ephesians 2:21

"At the present time your plenty will supply what they need, so that in turn their plenty will supply what you need."
2 Corinthians 8:14

"The body is a unit, though it is made up of many parts; and though all its parts are many, they form one body. So it is with Christ. For we were all baptized by one Spirit into one body- whether Jews or Greeks, slave or free -- and we were all given the one spirit to drink."
1 Corinthians 12:12

"Instead, speaking the truth in love, we will in all things grow up into him who is the head, that is, Christ.

From him the whole body, joined and held together by every supporting ligament, grows and builds itself up in love, as each part does its work."
Ephesians 4:15

"My purpose is that they may be encouraged in heart and united in love, so that they may have the full riches of complete understanding, in order that they may know the mystery of God, namely, Christ, in whom are hidden all the treasures of wisdom and knowledge."
Colossians 2:2

"For you were once darkness, but now you are light in the Lord. Live as children of light for the fruit of the light consists in all goodness, righteousness and truth."
Ephesians 5:8

Imagine that the majority of the people on Earth believe in God and have submitted their thoughts and wills to be in agreement with Him. James Redman refers to a similar concept of a set number of likeminded believers as the "critical mass" in his book *The Celestine Prophesy.* 7

When the majority of the people are of the same mindset and beliefs, then the shift of the world as we know it will occur. Psychologists call this concept "groupthink." In sales, it has similarly been called the "tipping point." 8 The Internet calls it "trending." 9

In any case, it is, in essence, when the weight of "the many" causes a shift in balance and the belief of the majority manifests. The Bible discusses this idea quite a bit. At the end of days, there will be a major shift in everything that we know. It will occur when the critical mass of believers have all heard and come to believe at exactly the time God said it would occur. We are getting to that point. Christianity is growing in leaps and bounds. There are now billions of Christians spreading the good news of God's love for all who die to themselves and become a part of this new life. With the Internet and the ease of information exchange being like no other generation before, this message is spreading on a global level. My friends, we are going to get there, whether you choose to believe or not. It is a force beyond our control. All we can do is decide whether we too will become a part of God's kingdom.

But remember: Once that time arrives, only those who have already become a part of God's righteousness will live on.

"If we died with him, we will also live with him."
2 Timothy 2:11

"If we have been united with him like this in his death, we will certainly also be united with him in his resurrection."
Romans 6:5

"Lift up your eyes to the heavens, look at the Earth beneath: the heavens will vanish like smoke, the Earth will wear out like a garment, and its inhabitants die like flies. But my salvation will last forever, my righteousness will never fail."
Isaiah 51:6

"In the beginning, O Lord, you laid the foundations of the Earth, and the heavens are the work of your hands. They will perish, but you remain; they will

all wear out like a garment. You will roll them up like a robe; like a garment they will be changed. But you remain the same, and your years will never end."
Hebrews 1:10

"May the God who gives endurance and encouragement give you a spirit of unity among yourselves as you follow Christ Jesus, so that with one heart and mouth you may glorify the God and Father of our Lord Jesus Christ."
Romans 15:5

"All of the believers were one in heart and mind."
Acts 4:32

"For you were once darkness, but now you are light in the Lord."
Ephesians 5:8

We could spend our whole life trying to figure out and understand all of the nuances of God's creation. Quantum physics, brain research, stem cell research, solar energy, metabolic energy, evolution, genetic decoding, cloning, astronomy, chemistry, heart disease, cancer, global warming, black holes, the psychology of war, fight or flight responses – where do the all the questions begin and end?

We cannot possibly understand everything. But we don't have to know it all. Our loving Father in heaven has given us Jesus. All we have to do is have faith in Him.

"You cannot solve problems with the same level of consciousness that created them." - Albert Einstein

"For God so loved the world that he gave his one and only Son that whoever believes in him shall not perish but have eternal life."
John 3:16

"For you were once darkness, but now you are light in the Lord."
Ephesians 5:8

By our faith, we can overcome the world and be saved. We can choose to replace the toxic, twisted energy that comes from the words of this fallen world with the energy of love that is God's word, Jesus.

We can begin now by allowing our hearts to be cleansed of everything that was not of God, and let them instead become full of grace and truth and love. We can live each day progressing in sanctification and continuing the development of our holy character in the same frequency as Christ.

Doctors have now observed that in many ways, our bodies have a way of somehow resetting themselves daily. Our cells, our baroreceptors, our associations all have somewhat of a baseline one day, then adapt to whatever we do that day, creating a new baseline for the next. With each day we can make choices that make us healthier the next. We can halt negative cycles in their tracks and cut off every pretension that sets itself up against God, and replace it with the truth – the Word of God – and change our associations, and heal our individual bodies and our collective beliefs.

From Jesus: **"Then he said to them all: "Whoever wants to be my disciple must deny themselves and take up their cross daily and follow me." Luke 9:23**

As you follow Him I encourage you to let His light overflow in you so that your face can shine, emitting all of the Glory of the Face of God.

"No one lights a lamp and puts it in a place where it will be hidden, or under a bowl. Instead he puts it on its stand, so that those who come in may see the light."
Luke 11:33

I would be remiss if I didn't take this opportunity to allow those who haven't yet, a moment of silence to repent and turn away from whatever used to lead you, and to invite Jesus in to save you and guide you back to life.

...

Jesus taught that at any given moment the past could be wiped clean; you could be a clean slate right now – where all things are possible with God.

We can count the blessings we awake with everyday and work forward from there, following the truth of God's word as we become disciplined, righteous and holy.

"Therefore consider carefully how you listen. Whoever has will be given more; whoever does not have, even what he thinks he has will be taken from him."
Luke 8:18

If you have chosen to become a part of Christ, and you do believe, I thank God for you, and encourage you to let your light shine. And, as my former pastor would say, "All of heaven is going nuts!" – cheering and celebrating the arrival of one of God's lost children. 10

Now to him who is able to establish you by my gospel and the proclamation of Jesus Christ, according to the revelation of the mystery hidden for long ages past, but now revealed and made known through the prophetic writings by the command of the eternal God, so that all nations might believe and obey him -- to the only wise God be glory forever through Jesus Christ.
     Romans 16:25

Epilogue: "The Time Is Now"

Now, after having completed this book, I feel compelled to reiterate the message that God has continued to urge me to share with you. He has made me keenly aware that the time is coming when, in an instant, our spirits will either become a part of the kingdom of God or will be left to suffer the wrath. And that time is near.

The end of time as we know it will happen so quickly that we will not have the opportunity to choose – at that time. We will either be ready, or we will miss it. There will be no time for us to consider our options, to rationalize, or to make the decision. The decision will already be made.

We are deceived if we think we will have the time then to humble ourselves, to admit our selfish ways, to own up to our self-serving plans and ask God for forgiveness. There won't be time then. The end is going to come so quickly that we won't have time to pause, reflect, and to recognize that we have spent our whole lives serving ourselves and feeding our earthly appetites, only to find out that our "selves" won't be remaining in the eternal life and that therefore all of our efforts have been for nothing.

We will have the sudden understanding then that we merely ran a rat race, striving for worldly treasures that are now completely meaningless.

So, the time to open our eyes to these truths and to humble ourselves to our Creator is NOW.

"Do not love the world or anything in the world. If anyone loves the world, the love of the Father is not in him. For everything in the world -- the cravings of sinful man, the lust of his eyes and the boasting of what he has and does -- comes not from the Father but from the

world. The world and its desires pass away, but the man who does the will of God lives forever."
1 John 1:15

"What good is it for a man to gain the whole world, and yet lose of forfeit his very soul?"
Luke 9:24

Without waking up now, we will have wasted all of our energy, completely missing the whole point and purpose of our lives. Worrying about our image here, our significance to others here, our success here, or what anyone else here thinks of us will become of no importance when the world as we know it crumbles, and the only thing remaining is God and all those souls who have become a part of His plan.

Just like the studies of brain activity that show the decisions we make are made for us before we are consciously aware, based on our brains overall assessment of billions of bits of information and how that information lines up with our goals and with what we have deemed to be important, our decision as to where our souls will belong is made before we will have the conscious choice. We have to learn ahead of time what is truly important, and know where our hearts should be.

God has repeatedly shown us in His word that this instantaneous burst of Christ on the scene of our Earth will come when we are not expecting it. If we want a warning signal or a sign to somehow indicate to us that the end of all things as we know it is coming so we will know that it is time to get ready, consider *this* it.

His very loud tug on me to write this book and the steps he took to ensure that I accomplished it are signs in themselves. He has been patient, not wanting anyone to perish, but the end time *is* coming. And only those who have *already* chosen to believe, and who have *already* made the decision to be a part of His kingdom, will get to live on.

Whoever is still entangled with the world and its possessions will be left behind to be condemned with the Earth. God's word repeatedly tells us the end will close on us unexpectedly.

Do not be fooled into thinking that you will have time to repent of the ways in which you rejected God and justified your actions for yourself. If anything I have said remains with you, let it be this: Today, right now, is the time to seek the truth. There is nothing more important.

"I tell you the truth: This generation will certainly not pass away until all these things have happened. Heaven and earth will pass away, but my words will never pass away. Be careful, or your hearts will be weighed down with dissipation, drunkenness and the anxieties of life, and that day will close on you unexpectedly like a trap. For it will come upon all those who live on the face of the whole earth.

Be always on the watch, and pray that you may be able to escape all that is about to happen, and that you may be able to stand before the Son of Man."
Luke 21:32

Recently, as I was praying to our Heavenly Father about a mistake I felt I had made, during my prayer I was led to that last passage over and over. I knew what He meant by "drunkenness and the anxieties of life," but I decided to look up the word "dissipation." I wanted to know how it was defined. I figured that since God had continued leading me to this scripture, I should take the time to find out its real meaning.

If you have read the last few chapters, you won't be surprised to hear what I read on *Wikipedia*: that in physics, *dissipation* represents the concept of mechanical models such as *waves* or oscillations, losing energy over time, typically as a result of friction or turbulence. In other words, God was saying to me, "Watch your wavelength."

I had been worried, and was not operating on the same wavelength as Christ. Had He come that minute, His energy would not have been transferred to me as I was not vibrating on His same frequency.

Even when things get rough, we have to stay clothed in Christ, and keep love as the driving force in our hearts. Remember His example, where even in His highest degree of suffering, and even to the point of death, He was still praying to God for the forgiveness of those around Him.

Although it seems cliché now, so many have said things like, "Let love be your guide," "Operate on love," "Just love each other," and etcetera, after seeing the science and scripture behind this, we can understand why it is truly important that we do these things. We must wake up to what is driving and motivating us, and keep it in check. Remember, whatever you are feeding your cells is what will be driving you for more. Are your cells being fed the bread of life? Scripture urges us over and over to love God, love our friends, love our neighbors, and even love our enemies.

Sometimes we try so hard to set ourselves up for a great life here, and to make this life so perfect, when the truth is that: **None of it matters**. The real life that is awaiting us is right around the corner. When Christ comes again, anyone who has not overcome the lures of the world will, according to God's words, suffer horribly in the final wrath. While they focus on indulging themselves here in this life, they will end up shut out of the most amazing feast and reunion ever dreamt of – one that will last for eternity. An amazing place I feel fortunate to have caught a glimpse of.

But those who are ready to go – clothed in peace, humility, love and the essence of Christ – will get to take part in the eternal life that truly matters.

This is why Jesus said:

"Blessed are the poor in spirit,
  for theirs is the kingdom of heaven.
Blessed are those who mourn,
  for they will be comforted.
Blessed are the meek,
  for they will inherit the earth.
Blessed are those who hunger and thirst for righteousness,
  for they will be filled.
Blessed are the merciful,
  for they will be shown mercy.
Blessed are the pure in heart,
  for they will see God.
Blessed are the peacemakers,
  for they will be called children of God.
Blessed are those who are persecuted because of righteousness,
  for theirs is the kingdom of heaven.

Blessed are you when people insult you, persecute you and falsely say all kinds of evil against you because of me. Rejoice and be glad, because great is your reward in heaven, for in the same way they persecuted the prophets who were before you." Matthew 5

"Our Savior has appointed two kinds of resurrection in the Apocalypse. 'Blessed is he that hath part in the first resurrection,' for such come to grace without the judgment. As for those who do not come to the first, but are reserved unto the second resurrection, these shall be disciplined until their appointed times, between the first and the second resurrection." 11

"But our citizenship is in heaven. And we eagerly await a Savior from there, the Lord Jesus Christ, who, by the power that enables him to bring everything under his control, will transform our lowly bodies so that they will be like his glorious body. There for my brothers, you whom I love and long for, my joy and crown, that is how you should stand firm in the Lord, dear friends!"

Philippians 3:20- 4:1

"Because of the increase of wickedness, the love of most will grow cold, but he who stands firm to the end will be saved." Matthew 24:12

"The righteous will live by faith."

Romans 1:17

"They will see his face, and his name will be on their foreheads."

Revelations 22:4

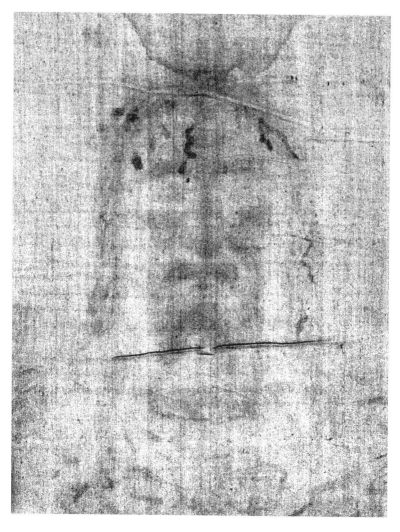

"… a copy and shadow of what is in heaven."

Hebrew 8:5

The Face of God 213

For nearly 2000 years, the image on the blood stained cloth called the Shroud of Turin had only been seen like that.

But in the darkroom in 1978, for the first time we were able to see the photoelectric effect that occurred as the powerful burst of light emanating from Jesus at the time of His resurrection altered the molecular structure of the cloth, leaving hidden within its fibers the image of the face of our Lord, Jesus Christ.

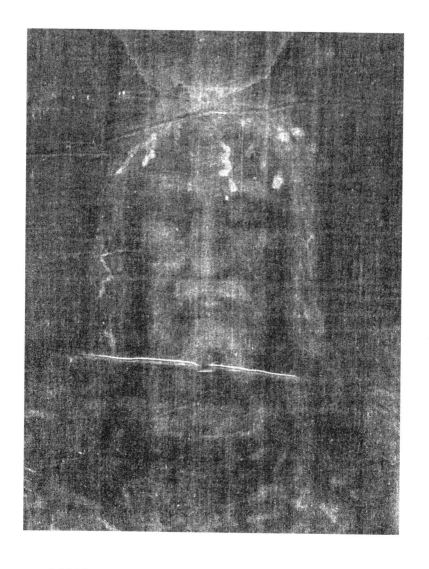

Notes

Introduction

1. *What the Bleep Do We Know?* DVD, directed by Mark Vincent, Betsy Chasse, and William Arntz (2004; Los Angeles, CA: 20th Century Fox, 2005).

Chapter 1

1. "Nikola Tesla," *Wikipedia*, http://en.wikipedia.org/wiki/Nikola_Tesla.
2. "Nikola Tesla—Master of Lightning," *AmericanBuilt.us*, http://americanbuilt.us/library/nikola-tesla.shtml.
3. Andy Stanley, senior pastor of North Point Community Church in Atlanta Georgia (sermon).

Chapter 2

1. *Bruce Almighty*, DVD, directed by Tom Shadyac (2003; Los Angeles, CA: Universal Studios, 2003).
2. *Questions and Answers about Memories of Childhood Abuse*, American Psychological Association, 1995.

3. Karl S. Kruszelnicki, "21 Grams," *ABC Science,* May 13, 2004, http://www.abc.net.au/science/articles/2004/05/13/1105956.htm.

4. Frank B. McMahon, Judith W. McMahon, and Tony Romano, *Psychology and You* (Saint Paul: West Publishing Company, 1990).

5. *What the Bleep Do We Know?* DVD, directed by Mark Vincent, Betsy Chasse, and William Arntz (2004; Los Angeles, CA: 20th Century Fox, 2005).

6. Frank B. McMahon, Judith W. McMahon, and Tony Romano, *Psychology and You* (Saint Paul: West Publishing Company, 1990).

7. Frank B. McMahon, Judith W. McMahon, and Tony Romano, *Psychology and You* (Saint Paul: West Publishing Company, 1990).

8. Frank B. McMahon, Judith W. McMahon, and Tony Romano, *Psychology and You* (Saint Paul: West Publishing Company, 1990).

9. Diane Ackerman, *An Alchemy of Mind: The Marvel and Mystery of the Brain* (New York: Simon & Schuster, 2004).

10. Frank B. McMahon, Judith W. McMahon, and Tony Romano, *Psychology and You* (Saint Paul: West Publishing Company, 1990).

11. "Cosmic Chemistry: Cosmogony," *Genesis: Search for Origins,* NASA, Jet Propulsion Laboratory, California Institute of Technology, http://genesismission.jpl.nasa.gov/educate/scimodule/Cosmogony.html.

Chapter 3

1. *What the Bleep Do We Know?* DVD, directed by Mark Vincent, Betsy Chasse, and William Arntz (2004; Los Angeles, CA: 20th Century Fox, 2005).
2. Candace Pert, Ph.D., *What the Bleep Do We Know?* DVD, directed by Mark Vincent, Betsy Chasse, and William Arntz (2004; Los Angeles, CA: 20th Century Fox, 2005).
3. Joe Dispenza, D.C., *What the Bleep Do We Know?* DVD, directed by Mark Vincent, Betsy Chasse, and William Arntz (2004; Los Angeles, CA: 20th Century Fox, 2005).
4. Wayne Purdin, "Serotonin Rising, sungazing and becoming a sun," *Examiner.com*, September 25, 2009, http://www.examiner.com/alternative-religions-in-national/serotonin-rising-sungazing-and-becoming-a-sun#ixzz1bBiF3Xrk.
5. "Oxytocin: The Hormone of Love," *Oxytocin.org*, http://www.oxytocin.org/oxytoc/.
6. Michael Kosfeld, Markus Heinrichs, Paul J. Zak, Urs Fischbacher, and Ernst Fehr, "Oxytocin Increases Trust in Humans," *Nature* 435 (June 2, 2005): 673-676, http://www.nature.com/nature/journal/v435/n7042/abs/nature03701.html.
7. Walter Greiner, *Quantum Mechanics: An Introduction* (Berlin: Springer, 2001),

http://books.google.com/?id=7qCMUfwoQcAC&pg=PA29&dq=wave-particle+all-particles.

8. Frank B. McMahon, Judith W. McMahon, and Tony Romano, *Psychology and You* (Saint Paul: West Publishing Company, 1990).

9. As recalled from an upper level psychology course taught at Virginia Tech.

10. Masaru Emoto and Tokujiro Kawasaki, *The Message from Water* (Tokyo: Hado Kyoikusha, 2004).

11. Rick Warren, *The Purpose Driven Life* (Michigan: Zondervan, 2002).

12. Don G. Campbell, *The Mozart Effect: Tapping the Power of Music to Heal the Body, Strengthen the Mind, and Unlock the Creative Spirit* (New York: Avon, 1997).

13. "Seratonin: The Chemistry of Well-Being." *Angelfire*, http://www.angelfire.com/hi/TheSeer/seratonin.html.

14. Wayne Purdin, "Serotonin Rising, sungazing and becoming a sun," *Examiner.com*, September 25, 2009, http://www.examiner.com/alternative-religions-in-national/serotonin-rising-sungazing-and-becoming-a-sun#ixzz1bBiF3Xrk.

15. Harold G. Koenig and Michael E. McCullough, *Handbook on Religion and Health* (Oxford: Oxford University Press, 2001).

16. "Tendency," definition, *Dictionary.com*, http://dictionary.reference.com/browse/tendency.

17. "Brain Scans Can Reveal Your Decisions 7 Seconds Before You 'Decide'," *Exploring the Mind*, http://exploringthemind.com/the-mind/brain-scans-can-reveal-your-decisions-7-seconds-before-you-decide.

Chapter 4

1. "Butterfly Effect," *Wikipedia,*
   http://en.wikipedia.org/wiki/Butterfly_effect.
2. "Copenhagen Interpretation," *Wikipedia,*
   http://en.wikipedia.org/wiki/Copenhagen_interpretati
   on.
3. Joe Dispenza, D.C., *What the Bleep Do We Know?*
   DVD, directed by Mark Vincent, Betsy Chasse, and
   William Arntz (2004; Los Angeles, CA: 20th
   Century Fox, 2005).
4. "Spirit," *Wikipedia,*
   http://en.wikipedia.org/wiki/Spirit.
5. "Spirit," definition, *Dictionary.com,*
   http://dictionary.reference.com/browse/spirit.
6. "Oxytocin," *Colorado State University,*
   http://www.vivo.colostate.edu/hbooks/pathphys/endo
   crine/hypopit/oxytocin.html.
7. As recalled from an advanced psychology course
   taught by Robin Pannenton, Ph.D., Psychology
   Department, Virginia Polytechnic Institute and State
   University.

Chapter 6

1. Tim Folger, "Top 100 Science Stories of 2007,"
   Discover, January, 2008: 45.

2. Skip Moen, Kenneth H. Blanchard, and Phil Hodges, *Words to Lead By: A Practical Daily Devotional on Leading Like Jesus*, (Tulsa, OK: Insight Publishing Group, 2005).
3. Tim Folger, "Top 100 Science Stories of 2007." *Discover*, January, 2008: 45.
4. Diane Ackerman, *An Alchemy of Mind: The Marvel and Mystery of the Brain* (New York: Simon & Schuster, 2004).

Chapter 7

1. Kenneth Silber, "MIND Reviews: Drive: The Surprising Truth about What Motivates Us," *Scientific American*, May 7, 2010, http://www.scientificamerican.com/article.cfm?id=mind-reviews-drive-the-surprising-truth.
2. "Hypnosis," *Wikipedia*, http://en.wikipedia.org/wiki/Hypnosis.
3. "Hypnosis & Surgery," *ScienCentral Archive*, October 1, 2004, http://www.sciencentral.com/articles/view.php3?type=article&article_id=218392369.
4. "Matching Images of Brain Activity with Complex Thought," *Science Debate*, August 31, 2011, http://www.sciencedebate.com/science-blog/matching-images-brain-activity-complex-thought.
5. "Researchers Tune into What Brain Hears," *ABC Science*, February 1, 2012.

http://www.abc.net.au/science/articles/2012/02/01/3419795.htm.

6. Don G. Campbell, *The Mozart Effect: Tapping the Power of Music to Heal the Body, Strengthen the Mind, and Unlock the Creative Spirit*, (New York: Avon, 1997).

7. Don G. Campbell, *The Mozart Effect: Tapping the Power of Music to Heal the Body, Strengthen the Mind, and Unlock the Creative Spirit*, (New York: Avon, 1997).

8. As recalled (possibly from the Osceola Regional Hospital magazine).

9. Don G. Campbell, *The Mozart Effect: Tapping the Power of Music to Heal the Body, Strengthen the Mind, and Unlock the Creative Spirit*, (New York: Avon, 1997).

10. Freeda Bowers, *Give Me 40 Days For Healing*, (Alachua, FL: Bridge-Logos Foundation, 2003).

11. Don G. Campbell, *The Mozart Effect: Tapping the Power of Music to Heal the Body, Strengthen the Mind, and Unlock the Creative Spirit*, (New York: Avon, 1997).

Chapter 8

1. Pastor Greg Dumas, Lead Pastor of The Crossing Church, Tampa, Florida (sermon).

2. Susan Kruglinski, "Top 100 Science Stories of 2007," *Discover*, January 2008: 56.

3. Robert Evans, "Particles Found to Break Speed of Light," *Reuters*, September 22, 2011,

http://www.reuters.com/article/2011/09/22/us-science-light-idUSTRE78L4FH20110922.

4. "Create Reality Using Your Thoughts—Scientifically Proven Methods," *Quantum Jumping*, http://www.quantumjumping.com/articles/parallel-universe/creating-reality/.

Chapter 9

1. Susan Kruglinski, "Top 100 Science Stories of 2007," *Discover*, January 2008: 56.
2. "Copenhagen Interpretation," *Wikipedia*, http://en.wikipedia.org/wiki/Copenhagen_interpretation.
3. "Quantum Entanglement," *Wikipedia*, http://en.wikipedia.org/wiki/Quantum_entanglement.
4. *What the Bleep Do We Know?* DVD, directed by Mark Vincent, Betsy Chasse, and William Arntz (2004; Los Angeles, CA: 20th Century Fox, 2005).
5. "Max Planck, Quotes," *Good Reads*, http://www.goodreads.com/author/quotes/107032.Max_Planck.
6. *Louie Giglio: How Great is Our God*, DVD, (Roswell, GA: Six Step Records, 2009).
7. *What the Bleep Do We Know?* DVD, directed by Mark Vincent, Betsy Chasse, and William Arntz (2004; Los Angeles, CA: 20th Century Fox, 2005).
8. Dan Vergano, "Future Holds Key to Quantum Physics," *USA TODAY*, November 21, 2010, http://www.usatoday.com/tech/science/columnist/vergano/2010-11-21-physics-future_N.htm.

Chapter 10

1. "Photoelectric Effect," *Wikipedia*, http://en.wikipedia.org/wiki/Photoelectric_effect.
2. John C. Iannone, *The Image and The Rose*, (Kissimmee, FL: North Star Production Studios, LLC, 2007).
3. "Copenhagen Interpretation of Quantum Mechanics," *Stanford Encyclopedia of Philosophy*, January 24, 2008, http://plato.stanford.edu/entries/qm-copenhagen/.
4. "Subatomic Particle," *Wikipedia*, http://en.wikipedia.org/wiki/Subatomic_particle.
5. Candace Pert, Ph.D., *What the Bleep Do We Know?* DVD, directed by Mark Vincent, Betsy Chasse, and William Arntz (2004; Los Angeles, CA: 20th Century Fox, 2005).
6. Candace Pert, Ph.D., *What the Bleep Do We Know?* DVD, directed by Mark Vincent, Betsy Chasse, and William Arntz (2004; Los Angeles, CA: 20th Century Fox, 2005).
7. Pastor Roland Buck, "You Are Covered (Atonement)," *Angels on Assignment*, http://www.angelsonassignment.org/atonement.html.

Chapter 11

1. "Resonance," *Wikipedia*, http://en.wikipedia.org/wiki/Resonance.
2. "Resonance," *Wikipedia*, http://en.wikipedia.org/wiki/Resonance.
3. "Natural Frequency and Resonance," College of Engineering and Computer Science, Wright State University, http://www.cs.wright.edu/~jslater/SDTCOutreachWebsite/nat_frequency.htm.
4. *The NIV Study Bible* (Grand Rapids, MI: Zondervan Publishing. House, 1995).
5. "Mechanical Resonance," *Wikipedia*, http://en.wikipedia.org/wiki/Mechanical_resonance.
6. "Resonance," *Wikipedia*, http://en.wikipedia.org/wiki/Resonance.
7. "Consecrate," definition, *Dictionary.com*, http://dictionary.reference.com/browse/consecrate.
8. "Repent," definition, *Merriam-Webster Online*, http://www.merriam-webster.com/dictionary/repent.
9. "Extraordinary Optical Transmission," *Wikipedia*, http://en.wikipedia.org/wiki/Extraordinary_optical_transmission.
10. "Photoemission Spectroscopy," *Wikipedia*, http://en.wikipedia.org/wiki/Photoemission_spectroscopy.

Chapter 12 and Epilogue

1. Valerie Greene, *Conquering Stroke: How I Fought My Way Back and How You Can Too*, (Hoboken, NJ: Wiley, 2008).
2. "Thought Experiment," *Wikipedia*, http://en.wikipedia.org/wiki/Thought_experiment.
3. "Thought Experiment," *Wikipedia*, http://en.wikipedia.org/wiki/Thought_experiment.
4. MapQuest, http://www.mapquest.com/.
5. "Homologous Recombination." *Wikipedia, the Free Encyclopedia*, http://en.wikipedia.org/wiki/Homologous_recombination.
6. Johnathon Pollusa, "Homologous Recombination of Double Strand Breaks," *YouTube*, June 8, 2010, http://www.youtube.com/watch?v=9PEdqBuDMHM.
7. James Redfield, *The Celestine Prophecy: An Adventure*, (New York: Warner, 1993).
8. Malcolm Gladwell, *The Tipping Point: How Little Things Can Make a Big Difference*, (Boston: Little, Brown, 2000).
9. *Trending Now*, Yahoo.com.
10. Pastor Joe Saragusa, former Lead Pastor at Celebrate Church in Celebration, Florida (sermon).
11. "Ambrose," *Wikipedia*, http://en.wikipedia.org/wiki/Ambrose.

*Photographs of the Shroud of Turin by licensed agreement courtesy of Barrie Schwortz, President of STERA, Inc., and the 1978 Barrie M. Schwortz Collection, STERA, Inc.

*For more information on the authenticity of the Shroud of Turin, see the making of the film, *The Image and The Rose*, by North Star Productions, at facebook.com/imageandtherose.

*For more information on music and healing visit musicforthesoul.org.

* *The FOG, The Face Of* God has a Facebook page for fans to like and make comments at: www.Facebook.com/pages/The-FOG-The-Face-of-God

*Or visit the author's blog at: www.TheFOGcenter.blogspot.com

Thank you. Keeping you in my prayers…
In Christ,
Sherry

The Face of God 230

14384800R00122

Made in the USA
Lexington, KY
25 March 2012